Lex Naturalis

A Journal of Natural Law   Volume 3   Spring 2018

Copyright © 2018
Pace University Press
41 Park Row, 15th Floor
New York, NY 10038

ISBN: 978-1-935625-26-1
ISSN: 2474-8994

Walter Raubicheck
Editor

Editorial Board

Harold Brown
Department of Philosophy & Religious Studies, Pace University

Michael Baur
Department of Philosophy, Fordham University

James M. Jacobs
Notre Dame Seminary, New Orleans

Gregory J. Kerr
Department of Philosophy & Theology, DeSales University

Robert Chapman
Department of Philosophy and Religous Studies, Pace University

Alice Ramos
Department of Philosophy, St. John's University

Peter Widulski
School of Law, Pace University

Lex Naturalis

CONTENTS

VOLUME 3   SPRING 2018

Editor's Note	Walter Raubicheck	1
FEATURED ARTICLES		
Wendell Berry and the Metaphysics of Traditional Natural Law	Nathan Metzger	5
An Exploration of the Role of Inclination in the Promulgation of the Natural Law	James M. Jacobs	31
Do Friends Need Justice or Do the Just Need Friendship? Natural Law as the Foundation for Justice and Friendship	Scott Jude Roniger	57
On an Alleged Tension in the *Catechism of the Catholic Church*	Christopher Tollefsen	85
Bartolomé de las Casas and the Long and Very Long, and Short and Very Short, History of Human Rights	Paul J. Cornish	111

BOOK REVIEWS

Review of *Philosophical Essays*　　Matthew Minerd　　137
Concerning Human Families
by Stanley Vodraska
(University Press of America, 2014)

Review of *Ethics in the Conflicts of*　　James G. Hanink　　143
Modernity: An Essay on Desire,
Practical Reasoning, and Narrative
by Alasdair MacIntyre
(Cambridge University Press, 2016)

CONTRIBUTORS　　147

CALL FOR PAPERS　　149

Editor's Note

    Lex Naturalis is a continuation of the journal *Vera Lex*, published by Pace from 1980 till 2010, which at its inception proclaimed that it was supported by the Natural Law Society and was an International Review on a Global Subject. It was begun and edited by Virginia Black, a Pace philosophy professor, and proved to be a successful publication that featured articles on all aspects of natural law theory by both academics and lawyers. As the first issue proudly stated,

> The Natural Law Society was founded in Basel, Switzerland, August 1979. Its purpose is to subject to critical examination the question of the existence of natural law and natural right, and their content and purpose. The Society is dedicated to strengthening the development of natural law/right philosophy and to understanding the relations between morals and the positive laws of nations and peoples. *Vera Lex*, the Society's review, was established to –
>
> Communicate and dialogue on the subject of natural law and natural right and to spread the education of natural law philosophy into the mainstream of contemporary thought.
>
> Clarify and bring up to date its supporting ideas and to meet opposing argument with consistency and scholarly integrity;
>
> Strengthen the current revived interest in the discussion of morals and law and advance its historical research.[1]

The Society took as its motto Cicero's statement that "[t]rue law (vera lex) is right reason in agreement with nature; it is of universal application, unchanging and everlasting...."

    Several contributors to *Lex Naturalis*, the current natural law journal published by the Pace University Press, are interested in reviving the Natural Law Society that sponsored the original journal. We believe that at this moment in American and world history the time is right for like-minded individuals who believe natural law is central to the right ordering of both the individual and society to meet regularly to discuss their beliefs and ideas and to have a journal in which to publish them. A session of the new Natural Law Society was held at the ACPA conference in November, and we hope to sponsor another panel in San Diego this November.

In its early years the journal was open to wide range of natural law theories. Though it took its name from Cicero and one finds many references to Plato, Aristotle, and Aquinas, a good number of its articles highlighted the thought of Enlightenment thinkers, one whole issue in 1985 being devoted to the ethical thought of Vico. Yet it also certainly featured a strong Aristotelian/Thomistic strain, publishing a lead article by Henry Veatch, the well-known Georgetown philosopher, in its third issue. The Society was also originally quite international in character: Its founding members included scholars from Denmark, Spain, and France.

The first issues contained a regular set of columns that contained short articles on topics such as Natural Law Ontology, Natural Law Controversy, and Positive Law Criticism of Natural Law: Natural Law Criticism of Positive Law. The latter column contained an interesting series of critiques of natural law theory by legal positivists, which were then replied to by natural law professors. Of course, the journal featured book reviews of relevant texts, including in a 1982 issue a favorable review of John Finnis's influential *Natural Law and Natural Rights*. In a 1985 issue, future issues were announced as being devoted to topics such as Edmund Burke and the Natural Law, Is the Social Contract a Natural Law Concept?, Reducing Legal Realism to Natural Law, and From Natural Law to Natural Right.[2]

The Natural Law Society participated in a number of conferences in its early years, and the first Natural Law Society meeting was held in Mexico City on August 3, 1981. By the 2000s, the Society has ceased to function as an entity that met regularly, though *Vera Lex*, under the able editorship of Pace's Professor Robert Chapman, still identified itself as the *Journal of the International Natural Law Society*. A glance at the titles of articles published between 2001 and

2009 show that the journal covered topics from natural law theory in Eastern thought to the relation of natural law to American democracy and liberalism. One issue was dedicated to the work of Finnis, which shows that the journal was open to the latest developments in "new" natural law theory as well as its classical forms.

Lex Naturalis, the successor to *Vera Lex*, is endeavoring to continue the excellent work of that venerable publication, but now also hopes to resuscitate the Natural Law Society to give the journal context and support — and, most importantly, to help establish natural law theory as an important contemporary strand of philosophical ethics and as an ongoing source of positive law. We are hoping the Society will be a vibrant group that would like to meet periodically to share ideas and receive intelligent criticism and feedback. We also hope that the Society will serve as a forum for young scholars who are being trained in Aristotelian/Thomistic ethics but find it difficult to find outlets for discussion and that the Journal will do the same as an avenue for publication of these ideas and discussions.

Notes
1. Virginia Black, Vera Lex, vol. 1, no. 1. (1980), 4.
2. Virginia Black, *Vera Lex*, vol. 5, no. 1. (1985), 28.

Wendell Berry and the Metaphysics of Traditional Natural Law

Nathan Metzger

Introduction

In this paper, I will argue that one of the main reasons that traditional natural law[1] is a hard sell in the modern, industrialized world is because we are now epistemically alienated from nature's ubiquitous teleological processes, aims, and limitations, and therefore we fail to intuitively recognize the once obvious idea that objective norms derive from a normative, meaningful nature outside of our heads. The thesis that particular proscriptions and prescriptions derive from a "natural law" understanding of human norms has gone from pedestrian to offensive in proportion to our industrializing, digitizing, and urbanizing. Our modern outlook seems to be proof of a natural desire to draw continuity between ourselves and our environments: in a world saturated in accidental substances and bereft of organic agency, we have succumbed to the heresy of metaphysical reductionism, and seem content to live in our own heads. Indeed, even some philosophers who decry modern-day metaphysical naturalism have, in the guise of "new" natural law, eschewed what Alasdair MacIntyre famously referred to as our "metaphysical biology," appealing only to the contours of practical reason. While this is an unfortunate state of affairs, not all is lost. There are ways to get back on track. One such way is by following the advice of Wendell Berry. I want to suggest that Wendell Berry's agrarian ruminations can help epistemically situate ourselves in relation to the richer, visceral, and more mysterious philosophy of nature correctly assumed by traditional natural law theory.

It is often and rightly said that we live in a disenchanted world. We might initially and correctly unpack this idea by saying that we have accepted what James Barham has called the Mechanistic Consensus.[2] But we should go on to suggest that this mechanistic consensus is a product not just of the "winning out" of Newtonian mechanics and the concomitant abandonment of an Aristotelian story about substantial form, irreducible powers, and final cause, but also the natural result of modern man's move away from the family farm—that is, from *the land*. Since we are alienated from nature and surrounded by artifacts in our urban (and suburban) environments, a proper epistemic acclimation to the ubiquity of natural normativity and an understanding of man's *continuity* with this normativity is difficult to acquire, making the Mechanistic Consensus that much more (unnaturally) enticing. Today, our *osmosis* is not shaped, even in part, by the ways of the wild, let alone by domesticated ducks, cows, pigs, sheep, and chickens; nor is it shaped by our own interaction with soil, crops, weather, the seasons, or the stars above us. Rather, it is derived from a carefully contrived, artificial, urban environment of reducible and manipulable artifacts. At best, we see nature on our screensaver, and speak of chickens only when virtue-signaling our organic diet preferences. In fact, we do not even see the stars anymore.[3] Flannery O'Connor famously said that to live in the modern age is to "breathe in nihilism." This statement is not rhetorical: to be saturated in an environment of artifacts, as opposed to a world of plants and animals, is precisely to be epistemically alienated from objective purpose, aim, and end. It is far too easy to live in our heads, when the world around us exudes no inherent meaning anyway.

Yet we who live in industrialized environments can help to acclimate ourselves, or at least to understand why this acclimation is so difficult to obtain, by looking at some of the agrarian essays of Wendell Berry. Berry's agrarian-themed writing can serve as an illuminating extrapolation from the traditional natural law theorist's insistence that human normativity is continuous with natural normativity more generally. By meditating on Berry's description of the mysterious and purposeful forces of nature that sustain the work of traditional farm life (and in turn, a flourishing human life), we will be better able to understand why the opposite of a disenchanted nature is truly an *enchanted* one, why this enchanted conception of nature is the needed background condition of traditional natural law, and yet also why our industrial osmosis has been so epistemically alienating. Berry's writing can help us get clarification as to why those on the far side of the industrial revolution wrongly insist on rejecting the reality of immanent normativity in human nature.

In what follows, I will not spend time explicating Berry's own eloquent condemnations of practices and behaviors that most conservative "natural law" theorists also condemn, nor will I describe in detail his endorsements of traditional understandings of issues such as sex and the family. These specific analyses of Berry's thought have been expertly given by others.[4] Indeed, many thinkers have convincingly pointed to the "deeply conservative" strain of thought in Berry's writing, despite his own (perhaps ironic) avenues of publication.[5] Rather, I want to examine Berry's non-technical articulation of the needed metaphysical background conditions that make sense of traditional natural law, in tandem with my own (somewhat) technical examination of these same metaphysical starting points. By looking at what Berry says about the traditional agrarian *mode of understanding*, through my own more detailed "philosophical" examination of this same starting point, we can help epistemically situate *ourselves* in relation to the metaphysical background conditions of traditional natural law, despite living far from Berry's own Kentucky homestead.

Where Should We Place Philippa Foot's Plant?

Traditional natural law starts with a basic point about humanity's continuity with the whole of creation. Indeed, Philippa Foot famously said that in moral philosophy, it is important to begin by talking about plants.[6] Foot said we can speak credibly about natural human goodness, and therefore human natural *norms*, precisely because we can do the same for all flora and fauna. If a plant is given light and water, it will thrive. It will not thrive as much if it is given a deficient amount of these elements. From these basic natural *facts* about plants, we can posit a set of uncontentious natural *oughts* about plants. They are uncontentious because they are conditional oughts: insofar as we want a plant to thrive as a plant, it therefore ought to have access to water and light, relative to the sort of plant that it is. We can further say, without contention, that a plant is harmed, as a plant, if it is not able to get these things in sufficient quantity, relative to the sort of plant it is.

But the reason that plants have a real way to thrive, and therefore real natural oughts relative to their thriving, is not because of something especially interesting about plants, but rather because plants are part of the world of living things. In the case of bugs and animals, as opposed to algae and sunflowers, they will need to also *do* certain things if they are to live well according to their kind (of course, I do not mean to imply that a plant is an inert, passive agent: no doubt, a plant reaches and strives and seeks and, in the case of some plants, like sunflowers, actively turn directions; yet we colloquially use the word "rooted" to mean "stationary" for a reason). Like any fungus, dolphins need light and water. But dolphins, as moving subjects of experience, will thrive if (among other things) they swim correctly, cooperate with their pack, catch fish for themselves and their baby dolphins to eat, and teach their young how to be good dolphins in turn.[7] Not surprisingly, what is true of dolphins and plants will also be true, relative to their own natures, of ants and yaks. We should quickly note the exceptional explanatory power of Michael Thompson's brilliant talk of the "Aristotelian Categorical." He helpfully explains that when we speak of an animal having a particular feature, we are describing how that animal in fact *ought* to be a certain way, not that they necessarily are that way. Yaks have four legs, so they ought to have four legs. This is a true fact, and a true norm, about yaks. Neither this natural fact nor its derivative natural ought are falsified if you come upon a three-legged yak. It is only evidence of an unfortunate yak.[8]

Human beings are natural things. We are built of the same chemical stuff as worms, plants, dolphins, and yaks. We are a particularly interesting, yet earth-bound, biological animal—a clever one, no doubt; but we are part of a natural continuum of substantial forms. Yes, our rationality makes us (divinely) special, but we are formed from the same periodic table that produced yaks and salmon, and a million other things that yearn to thrive according to their kind. As Conor Cunningham describes our naturalness, we are not angels, and we are not Jedi Knights.[9]

To mention our continuity with the rest of nature is not to downplay our specialness, but instead to elevate the specialness of the non-rational world. Indeed, traditional natural law theory insists that while our rational agency makes us unique, our specialness is in many ways continuous with the specialness of all life, and indeed, all creation—both organic and inorganic. One here thinks of Hans Jonas' oft-quoted talk of the animal kingdom: "In the hue and cry over the indignity done to man's metaphysical status in the doctrine of animal descent, it was overlooked that by the same token some dignity had been restored to the realm of life as a whole. If man was the relative of animals, then animals were the relatives of man and in degrees bearers of that inwardness of which man, the most advanced of their kin, is conscious in himself."[10] Moreover, as Wendell Berry himself rightly points out in his essay *Getting Along with Nature*, "[t]he Chain of Being—which gave humans a place between animals and angels in the order of Creation—is an old idea that has not been replaced by any adequate new one. It was simply rejected, and the lack of it leaves us without a definition."[11] But to return to Foot's original idea, it is precisely the obviousness of our biological continuity that should allow us easily to posit that human norms should follow from our natures, analogously to how norms derive from the natures of every other substance in creation. That is to say, normativity does not emerge on the earthly scene with the creation of man's practical reason. It has been there all along: we humans merely live according to our particular (and no doubt quite interesting) version of it.

Indeed, precisely because we *are* so continuous with flora and fauna in so many ways, we will be able to find our norms not just by the hearth fire of "practical reason," but by feeling the soil and getting out of our heads. It is through a broader and richer conception of our biological being-in-the world, now considered as the rich, teleologically laden place that it is, that we find our norms. We can assume that some more general human oughts will be in common with those of plants and bugs, that some will also be in common with those of dolphins, and that some will be exclusively in common with those of our next-of-mammalian kin. We can also surmise that many human oughts will be unique to us, given that we are a uniquely rational animal. To be thriving, successful members of our kind, we will have to do certain things and avoid doing other things, relative to our human nature, and we will also need to have certain things happen to us and other things not happen to us, relative to this same nature.

Philippa Foot is right: it turns out that we *can* say quite a bit about human norms by extrapolating from plants. We can argue *to* the metaethical *reality* of objectively good and bad human behavior *from* an observation of how to properly treat a plant. But we should notice, again, that this is done not by isolating our intellects, but by entering the lived world of biological norms, from algae to whales.

The above is but one version of what is told in classrooms across the land when describing the metaphysical background condition needed for traditional natural law to get off the ground. But how *convincing* is this story—one which starts with facts about plants needing sunlight and ends with particular proscriptions and condemnations of objectively bad human behavior? It depends, I would contend, on where we place the plant. William Ophuls, in his illuminating work *Plato's Revenge*, rightly reminds us that the specifics of our natural norms must be "reasonably discovered and not rationally proven." He goes on to argue that the reasonability of our discoveries will hinge first of all on our realization that we are part of nature, and not outside of it. That is, we must assume an ecological starting point. Indeed, to start with plants is to show that neither meaning, nor moral law, are found in the head. They are found only when we properly situate ourselves in and among a world teeming with natural agency.[12]

So let us consider this plant again. Picture our plant in a pot, on a window sill. We pull back our focus, and we notice that the window is situated fifty stories above the earth. Outside the window is a beautiful but endless complex of glass skyscrapers. Every which way we see artificial light—from windows, from digital billboards, from cars, and from planes. But not from the night sky. The faint dim of honking horns is heard on the streets below, punctuated by the ring of police sirens. Inside the window is an immaculate studio apartment. On one wall is a large flat screen television. On another, digital picture frames show an ever-changing array of digital images. On the table sits a laptop, an iPad, and an iPhone. The plant is one of three living things in the apartment. There is also a dog and the dog's adopter.

Now picture this same plant in the ground, in a country garden. We pull back our focus, and we see this plant surrounded by a hundred other plants, all rooted in rich topsoil stuffed with manure, pollen, and dead leaves. Outside the garden is a beautiful, endless complex of trees. From up above we see a thousand lights—the stars. The faint din of crickets and nightingales is heard from the forest, interspersed with the sounds of moos and clucks from the nearby barn. A small pen of sleeping hogs sits nearby. Next to the plant in the garden is a family of rabbits, trying to avoid the detection of a farmer checking on the cows. The land is saturated with life, from the rich top soil, to the crops, to the fallow fields nearby, to pasture land teeming with bugs of a hundred varieties, to the stables of horses, to sheep, to the family dog, to cows, dung, soil, fungus, and the occasional invading coyote.

Foot's invocation of plants is brilliant—and crucial. Yet I do not think that by pointing to the plant in the window sill of a high-rise apartment we will end up giving proper illumination to Foot's idea of *continuity*. In order to see our continuity with the rest of nature, we actually have to be in the thick of it.

Wendell Berry's Naïve Worldview

Like Foot, Wendell Berry talks a lot about plants and what they need to thrive. But he also mentions natural norms as they relate to animal husbandry, crop rotation, bird migration, good manure, good topsoil, birthing calves, bailing hay, making butter, slaughtering pigs, and growing trees. Berry's subjects are myriad, but broadly speaking, he writes with concern about the ways that modern industrial living and modern, reductionist fetishizations of nature compromise not just the traditional farm, and not just the environment as a whole, but more basically, our understanding of our place in nature. We might say, generally speaking, that Wendell Berry implores us to see how nature's ways should rightly shape our own. But Berry does this not through a philosophical treatise, but by describing the daily demands of life on the farm. For this reason, Berry's writing can help us better see not just why we need to abandon our default, mechanistic vision of reality, but, more importantly, just how brilliantly but mysteriously purposeful and even enchanted our natural world truly is. Just as importantly, Berry suggests why we who live in the world of artifacts have trouble seeing this same world. Berry words it well in his essay, *Six Agricultural Fallacies*: "[A]griculture deals with living things and biological processes, whereas the materials of industry are not alive and the processes are mechanical."[13] The consequences of industrial living, it seems, are an artifactual projection onto the natural world. What Berry concludes from this simple but crucial metaphysical insight, I contend, can help the proponents of traditional natural law explain their starting points.

Berry writes about how traditional farming methods are not just better for the animals, the soil, the surrounding land, the farming family, and the thriving of rural life, but ultimately for our own real flourishing. Thus, what Berry does, through his criticism of industrial farming, and his enthusiastic descriptions of traditional farming, is connect man with nature properly, by describing not just man's proper dependency on nature, but how man, as part of nature, is a deeply purposeful agent, through and through.

But again, one should not mischaracterize Berry's intent. Berry writes about farming. He writes about properly caring for animals. About shoveling manure. About healthy topsoil (no doubt a word cloud of Berry's essays would show TOPSOIL in the largest font size). Then again, precisely because his writing is so visceral and humdrum, one can properly see the teleological character of these farming activities. Indeed, despite writing about such mundane things like crop rotation, topsoil, and manure, Berry's writing is in fact a not-so-subtle endorsement of what political philosopher Michael Sandel, in a more specifically philosophical context, has endorsed as the "naïve" worldview. It is the worldview that insists on the ubiquitous reality of agency, irreducible powers, and purpose. It is the worldview that we see before theory—and more importantly, before industrial environments—get in the way. We should naturally see a world that exudes purpose and agency and we should see a world that refuses submission to mechanical explananda.

But we do not. Then again, a certain suspicion concerning nature's immanent agency is hard to school out of us, regardless of where we live. Rupert Sheldrake encapsulates the unnaturalness of the mechanistic consensus quite simply: "To many people, especially gardeners and people who keep dogs, cats, horses or other animals, it is blindingly obvious that plants and animals are living organisms, not machines."[14] James Barham is certainly on to something when he writes "[a]ccording to the Mechanistic Consensus, the things that happen in organisms do not really happen for a purpose; it only *looks* that way."[15] Michael Sandel also suggests, quite rightly, that this naive vision is what children do see until school gets in the way: "With the advent of modern science, nature ceased to be seen as a meaningful order....To explain natural phenomena in terms of purposes, meanings, and ends was now considered naive and anthropomorphic. Despite this shift, the temptation to see the world as teleologically ordered, as a purposeful whole, is not wholly absent. It persists, especially in children, who have to be educated out of seeing the world in this way."[16]

However, while these sentiments are noteworthy, they do not properly take account of the dramatic effects that our industrial environments can have on our intuitions. What Sandel writes about the "educating out" of the naive view is no doubt true, but we can imagine that a teacher's insistence that children abandon their more enchanted view of nature and accept the "scientific consensus" would be more efficacious in changing their minds if those children did not ever live on a small farm, but in a high-rise apartment, or even a large house in a modern residential neighborhood in a sprawling suburb. In fact, Berry reminds us that access to even a garden is not the norm, and for this reason we can be easily acclimated away from the naive view. The waning of the naive view is more broadly the consequence of industrial living. Whether or not one is explicitly taught to reject teleological understandings of nature and instead accept the mechanical consensus, it is simply harder to see when the natural world is spied only on a laptop, instead of at one's feet. Richard Louv, in his celebrated book *Last Child in the Woods*, has described how in the contemporary West, "nature is more abstraction than reality. Interestingly, nature is something to watch, to consume, to wear—to ignore."[17] Indeed, argues Louv, even children, who more naturally see purposeful nature as it truly is, have been so artificially alienated from nature that they view it with suspicion. And as Berry himself argues, children who grow up away from trees, animals, soil, fields, stars, and forests, and in particular, without a *labored engagement* through and with all of these aforementioned dynamic, natural meaningful forces, but who are instead enculturated into industrial forms of living—a form that is wholly reliant on artifactual engagement—can less easily gleam from nature its own objective purposes and ways of thriving. It stands to reason that these same children are therefore less able to see how nature can show us the standards of our own behavior—our virtues and vices, our proscriptions. For children on the far side of the industrial revolution, that which is natural—including the moral law itself—now seems alien.

The world of artifacts does not speak to us in the same way, precisely because artifacts (as will be shown next) have no immanent agency and purpose. What might be the metaethical consequence of this historically novel industrial acclimation? In order to answer that, we should get a better sense of what the rejection of the mechanistic consensus truly means, in order to see what its acceptance has allowed us to lose.

The Metaphysics of Enchantment

I have not shied away from using the term "enchantment" to describe the contours of our natural world. While such terminology invokes a fantastic, mysterious, and mystifying image of nature, we must realize that this is precisely what nature really is. When one truly rejects the heresy of the mechanical model, with its talk of blind and brute Newtonian bumping and banging, and one then becomes reconciled with the older, essentialist metaphysics of substantial forms with immanent aim and end—the very metaphysics that grounds traditional natural law—one is drawn back into our own fantastic world. As G.K. Chesterton once put it in *The Ethics of Elfland*, we need to see our own world with fresh eyes.

But how might we explain this epistemic reorientation more succinctly? Let us start by looking at some key metaphysical differences between natural substances and human artifacts. A thing built by human beings—an artifact—is composed of parts and is therefore reducible to those parts. An artifact has no powers that are not explainable by a mechanical emergence story involving these very parts. By contrast, a natural substance, whether organic or inorganic, is first of all an irreducible whole. As opposed to an artifact, a substance, as an irreducible whole, has powers and features that cannot be cashed out by way of a mechanical emergence story involving the parts that make it up. Substances have an irreducible unity, one might say. We might here invoke physicist P.W. Anderson's important phrase, *more is different*. Our move upward from weak and strong forces, to atoms, to molecules, to cells, to yaks, is ontologically to add to the world, due to the efficient powers of every irreducible level of existence and the way that they point to still higher levels. One interesting aspect of the essence of these substantial forms is that, as macro-level, irreducible wholes, they have a teleological component. They have form-specific aims and ends and form-specific tendencies to cause a range of activities and functions in the world. As David Oderberg writes, "the very concept of an essence or nature, whether that of a living or a non-living thing, carries with it the idea of a characteristic tendency towards a certain kind of operation or behaviour, and resistance to other kinds of behavior or causes contrary to the thing's nature."[18]

Thus, on the one hand we can say that hydrogen and oxygen point to the realization of water. On the other hand, we can say that water—cold and wet stuff—itself has irreducible powers: it is miscible with ethanol and immiscible with oil, and when it freezes, it makes the non-frozen water around it cold. To see how this older conception of essence differs from many modern accounts, let us recall the much celebrated essay by Hilary Putnam in which he asks us to imagine a "Twin Earth" where their water is not "identical" with H_2O, but instead to the chemical compound "XYZ." What should we think about this "possible-world" conundrum? Is Twin Earth water "identical" to Normal Earth water? The traditional essentialist responds that water is not "identical" to H_2O to begin with, so the question is moot. Water is irreducibly cold and wet stuff. It is realized by and structured by the irreducible efficient causal powers of hydrogen and oxygen atoms, but certainly cold and wet stuff is not identical to these two elements of the periodic table. So neither is Twin Earth water "identical" to the counter-factual atomic structure "XYZ."

Then again, thought experiments aside, the irreducible powers of water might not immediately turn heads, mysterious as they are. This is because, as David Oderberg words it, non-organic substances only exhibit transient teleology—or teleology that entirely points beyond itself. But with living substances, we see immanent teleological processes. Living substances, from ants to yaks, act for the well-maintenance of themselves and other living things. With living things, we can more easily invoke the language of purpose and agency, and a much more interesting normativity, to make sense of the striving, desiring activity of these substances.

Embryonic development, for example, shows us a clear example of immanent teleological activity: we should see here that neither organic nor inorganic substances are the result of mechanical motion: nothing in organic nature is merely blindly bumped from behind. Rather, a small, unified agent, composed and structured by various cells, divides and grows according to a latent goal—the entity seems to be pulled into the future through an infinite series of future (intentional) goals that it perpetually instantiates through its unfolding.[19] In the course of its development, it grows internal organs, which are themselves irreducible wholes with purposes relative to their own maintenance and development, but also relative to the highest-level whole—the embryo-to-fetus. But, of course, the maintenance of the highest-level whole in this series of nested wholes is directly relevant to any one of the lower-nested wholes. Thus the word "immanent" is helpful here. It helps remind us that these living processes and purposes are inherent to the living thing: they are the result of in-built agency—an agency in the irreducible, unified thing. The living unity self-repairs and self-organizes on multiple (irreducible) levels of its nested whole. Rupert Sheldrake puts the point well: "No machine starts from small beginnings, grows, forms new structures within itself and then reproduces itself."[20]

Indeed, the failure of the mechanistic consensus to properly describe nature, even inorganic nature (as was shown), but especially organic nature, is tacitly admitted even by some mechanists. Despite being ruled by the Mechanistic Consensus, biological descriptions are rife with promissory notes for a time when the language of agency will not have to be employed. James Barham puts the point well: "Although biologists may *say* that it is only a matter of convenience, the fact is that biological treatises and textbooks are saturated with teleological, normative, and even intentional terminology of every sort, and it would in fact be impossible to discuss the phenomena of life at all without recourse to such descriptors."[21]

The "hard problem" is everywhere: the world is saturated with irreducible wholes—and wholes within wholes—on both the level of the inorganic as well as organic. From the standpoint of what we could ever mechanically explain, the natural world is simply full of mystery from top to bottom. By comparison, artifacts are not unified wholes. As John Searle has famously shown, there is no mystery to a super computer.[22] It is, like a simple toaster, an accidental substance. It is composed of parts, its various powers are explainable by a mechanical emergence story, and it is reducible to parts. Our use of artifacts is relative to the desires of the user. We can use computers to send emails, but we can also use them as doorstops (the older models are good for little else). We can take them apart or add on to them. We can hack their contrived programs. Their (arbitrary) aim and end follow the accidental form given to it by the mechanic or artist or indeed the temporary user of the artifact. If, for the mechanist, art copies nature, then nature is reducible like artifacts. But if art imitates nature, whereby we can speak of the ontological divide between an artifact and a natural substance, then a contrived, industrial environment will exude significantly different metaphysical features than an environment saturated in myriad, organic life.

Having previously described the mysterious aspects of substantial wholes, we might now helpfully suggest that the famed naturalistic fallacy is simply the reasonable acknowledgment that there is indeed a cosmologically significant "hard problem" when it comes to establishing the background condition for natural law. After all, to point to irreducible causal powers and immanent aims and ends is in fact to point out that there is no unpacking nature's mystery. Since more is different, Laplace's demon meets dead ends constantly. From the standpoint of what could ever be logically explained or predicted, nature's powers, its ways of manifesting new substances and pointing to new features, and its ways of unfolding are forever beyond our ken. No doubt, by starting with Foot's plant, we can discover a myriad of natural ends and irreducible purposes, and therefore speak of nature's true and constant oughts, relative to the forms in question. But precisely because substances unfold and manifest new substances not because of blind, mechanical (and therefore predictive) emergence, but instead because of their irreducible causal powers, we therefore have to live in nature to absorb nature's meaning.

It would be wrong to say that there is no meaning simply because we cannot deduce it from an armchair, in the same way that it would be wrong for a farmer to stop tending to his orchard, merely because he recognizes, as Chesterton himself does in *The Ethics of Elfland*, that there is nothing logically necessary about a tree's irreducible powers to manifest fruit. To invoke William Ophuls again: we must reconcile with the fact that human norms must be "reasonably discovered" and that they cannot be "rationally proven." Hume is right, in one important sense, anyway. If causation is merely about what mechanically and predictively follows from what, then the power of trees to grow fruit is indeed mysterious. Our world, from top to bottom, is saturated in irreducible substances with irreducible powers. We just do not know it, because our environments prevent us from knowing it. For that reason, the naturalistic fallacy has power.

Wendell Berry on Disenchantment

Berry's criticisms of industrial farming, as well as his profound analyses of the mysterious forces and natural processes he observes and counts on when nurturing a successful small farm, can be easily understood by way of an Aristotelian conception of form, agency, and irreducible powers. More to the point, Berry's description of nature shows us here in the industrialized world not only why nature has norms, but also why a human being is part of this mysterious nature and must listen to it properly for the human being's own good.

Berry rails against reductionist analyses of nature (without, of course, invoking this sort of technical vocabulary), imploring his readers always to remember that nature contains powers and agencies that transcend what we could ever understand through a mere mechanical analysis. He reminds his readers that while we can, to our peril, reductively rearrange and itemize various components of the natural system for the sake of economic gain—for more milk, more yield, large chicken breasts, etc.—we cannot re-recreate nature, nor copy its irreducible powers. "Humans are intelligent enough to select for a type of creature," he writes in *Six Agricultural Fallacies*, "[but] they are not intelligent enough to *make* a creature."[23] He says the same thing about topsoil. In a pivotal essay called *Two Economies*, he argues, "We cannot speak of topsoil, indeed we cannot know what it is, without acknowledging at the outset that we cannot make it. We can care for it (or not), we can even, as we say, 'build' it, but we can do so only by assenting to, preserving, and perhaps collaborating with *its own* process [my emphasis]."[24] And soon after: "We cannot do what the topsoil does, any more than we can do what God does or what a swallow does."[25] When we "hack" the elements of nature, and treat these elements as reducible artifacts with predictive, mechanical causal elements, we give evidence of our profound misunderstanding of what nature in fact is, and in turn what we are capable of doing both to nature and (therefore) to ourselves. These passages from Berry's writing give evidence of the ways that art imitates but does not copy nature: the normativity of nature is immanent to it, since it is a product of the irreducible powers. Moreover, nature shows us that the irreducible powers of substance are experienced both on the organic and inorganic levels. Topsoil, no doubt, includes many living elements; but it also includes much that, while inorganic, still exudes a power that the mechanistic consensus fails to properly respect.

In fact, as previously mentioned, Berry constantly speaks of topsoil. He is clearly amazed at what we might more technically call soil's irreducible, efficient causal powers. He often argues that a failure to respect the mystery of something as prima facie mundane as topsoil has led to our ruin. In his essay *A Native Hill*, Berry writes, "The most exemplary nature is that of the topsoil. It is very Christ-like in its passivity and beneficence, and in the penetrating energy that issues out of its peaceableness. It increases by experience, by the passage of seasons over it, growth rising out of it and returning to it, not by ambition or aggressiveness. It is enriched by all things that die and enter into it. It keeps the past, not as a history or memory, but as richness, new possibility."[26] Soil then becomes a particularly instructive element; it is a mixture of the living, the dead, and the non-living. It shows the ways that transient and immanent teleological aspects are sometimes difficult to parse, and why the mechanistic consensus simply has no explanatory inroad.

Berry's reminders of nature's powers are therefore helpful to understanding the mysterious power of nature, and why nature—even something as humble as soil—sits not passively to the side of our rationality, but instead informs it. But that something as mundane as soil can inform our moral outlook shows just how important it is to not alienate humanity from the natural world. Given our alienation, therefore, we are far more likely to argue that human rationality and human happiness are ontologically distinct and liberated from nature, and that at the heart of this liberty is the right to define one's own concept of existence, of meaning, of the universe, and of the mystery of human life. Since, according to the mechanistic consensus, art copies nature, and since the world outside of our heads contains no immanent meaning, then nothing holds us back but our own whim. If human beings do not see themselves as creatures continuous with a world saturated with normativity, we will be far more likely to find our source of normativity through our own alienated and unnatural desires, and in the process, we will risk dividing ourselves against nature. As Berry words it, "to be divided against nature, against wildness, then, is a human disaster because it is to be divided against ourselves. It confines our identity as creatures entirely within the bounds of our own understanding, which is invariably a mistake because it is invariably reductive. It reduces our largeness, our mystery, to a petty and sickly comprehensibility."[27]

Berry reminds us that to live among a myriad of natural processes is to see how nature properly restrains us, and how our shaping, domesticating, and nurturing of nature must give deference to powers that we could never copy. Industrial living puts us outside the visual scope of nature's processes and purposes, and therefore alienates us from what Berry calls the "ancient definition" of the good—that our norms are found through nature that shows us powers that are more than we can mechanically explain. "Lacking that ancient definition, or any such definition," writes Berry, "we do not know at what point to restrain or deny ourselves. We do not know how ambitious to be, what or how much we may safely desire, when or where to stop."[28]

However, we should remember our initial invocation of plants when considering our place in nature. As we have shown, the human being is properly home in nature, but because he is rational, he is therefore quite different than other things in nature in a key way. As such, proper epistemic acclimation will mean living *well* within nature, while still acknowledging that man, precisely because of his rational nature, will nurture and change nature in some respects.

Wendell Berry speaks often of this tension. A major theme of his writing is the two sorts of mistakes that modern man makes when considering the role of the natural world. Both mistakes, he argues, come from an unnatural intuition about nature that is shaped by industrial living: namely, when we think of nature as a particularly beautiful artifact. Thus one mistake often made, which Berry suggests is more common on the "left," is to fetishize nature. The "environmentalist" argues that nature must be "preserved" in a state that sees no human interaction, on the assumption that nature is a sort of beautiful artifact, and that we should respect this artifact in the same way that we would a painting—by leaving it alone. Berry often argues that nature is fetishized precisely because industrialized environments have so little of this natural beauty in its own midst. He writes,"…the more artificial a human environment becomes, the more the word 'natural' becomes a term of value. It can be argued, indeed, that the conservation movement, as we know it today, is largely a product of the industrial revolution. The people who want clean air, clear streams, and wild forests, prairies, and deserts are the people who no longer have them."[29] What they have, alternatively, are ever more complicated artifacts that shape the contours of life and our understanding of it.

Another mistake, which Berry says happens more on the "right," is when modern man aggressively applies the consequences of the mechanistic consensus *to* nature, and particularly to food production. Just as an artifact can be reassembled and rearranged, just as programs can be hacked, so, we think, can the farm and its food be reassembled and reimagined, and its various living components—its soil, its animals, its fields—be mechanically "hacked" and controlled. Berry writes, "One of the favorite words of the industrial economy is 'control'…But, because we are always setting out to control something that we refuse to limit, we have made control a permanent and a helpless enterprise. If we will not limit causes, there can be no controlling of effects….More than anything else, we would like to 'control the forces of nature,' refusing at the same time to impose any limit on human nature. We assume that such control and such freedom are our 'rights,' which seems to ensure that our means of control (of nature and of all else that we see as alien) will be violent."[30] That is, modern man sees the growing of crops and the raising of cows and pigs and chickens as an extension of artifactual creation. The very notion of the "factory farm" is a consequence of seeing nature not as the home of fixed, irreducible forms—cows, pigs, topsoil, trees—but instead of the mechanical movement of reducible parts that can be hacked and rearranged for ever more efficiency, productivity, and economic value. Steve Talbott makes a similar point: "What the ecological conversation requires of us is to raise this dim sense, as best we can, to clear understanding. The question of what belongs to an animal or a plant or a habitat is precisely the question of wholeness and integrity. It is a question foreign and inaccessible to conventional thinking simply because we long ago quit asking it. We had to have quit asking it when we began feeding animal remains to herbivores such as cows, and when we began raising chickens, with their beaks cut off, in telephone book-sized spaces."[31]

Thus, Berry sees industrial farming as entirely consistent with the fetishizing of nature. Both views, we might say, conceive of nature as ontologically distinct from what could ever house immanent purpose. For this reason, one could hold to the idea that some parts of nature should stay pristine for our aesthetic enjoyment, but other parts should be mechanically exploited for economic gain. Berry writes, "The defenders of nature and wilderness—like their enemies the defenders of the industrial economy—sometimes sound as if the natural and the human were two separate estates, radically different and radically divided. The defenders of nature and wilderness sometimes seem to feel that they must oppose any human encroachment whatsoever, just as the industrialists often apparently feel that they must make the human encroachment absolute."[32] What is forgotten here is the idea broached by Foot's invocation of plants—that human beings are teleological agents in a teleological world, and continuous with that world. Or, as William Ophuls puts the point, "To accept that the human species is but one small part of an organic web of life that places fundamental constraints on our actions is bitter medicine indeed for the heirs of Bacon and Descartes. But it seems that we shall have to swallow the medicine nonetheless, abandoning the delusion of radical separation that fuels the illusion of unlimited mastery."[33] If we articulate natural law ecologically and not just via practical reason, we will better understand why elevating an individual over community makes little sense, and also why we must see nature as our ally and not think of the human being as *sui generis* lord over something alien. Yet, since we are alienated from nature, we do not easily see our own natural limits. This does real moral damage to us.

 As an alternative, Berry reminds us that we, as the particular sort of animals that we are, necessarily must tame and nurture nature for our own benefit, but that we must do so in a way that respects the natural processes of the nature we broach. Indeed, to do so is to properly access *our* own nature, and live according to it. We see the traditional family farm as particularly didactic, then, and a model of what traditional natural law is all about. It is an environment that is formed by a vast, but properly tamed and nurtured nature.

 So we should find it noteworthy, precisely because it serves as such an effective witness to the metaphysical coherence of traditional natural law theory, that the family farm has largely disappeared, having been replaced by large factory farms filled with hacked creatures, on land that has lost its rich topsoil to an erosion caused by misuse. Yet for our purposes, this mention of the degradation of the natural world, and in particular of the farm, is of *secondary* importance. We should note, more fundamentally, that our degradation of nature has not left the *human being* unscathed. Indeed, the destruction of the family farm has hastened the degradation of our own understanding of ourselves, of our morals, and of our very knowledge of morality. Traditional natural law has waned precisely because the family farm has waned. Both our fetishization and destruction of non-human nature has come concurrently with the destruction of our own moral knowledge.

Wendell Berry on the Importance of Experiencing Nature's Norms

As mentioned, Berry sees our both our fetishizing of nature, and (on the flipside of the same coin) the raw exploitation of nature, as a failure of properly seeing nature. Berry repeatedly emphasizes how we need to hone the scale of agricultural production precisely because it is only by directly experiencing this dynamic system that we allow for proper epistemic acclimation to the mystery and flow of this very system. To repeat: we cannot live in our heads; we have to feel the soil: "Everywhere, every day, local life is being discomforted, disrupted, endangered, or destroyed by powerful people who live, or who are privileged to think that they live, *beyond the bad effects of their bad work.*"[34] That is to say, we cannot understand nature's norms by simply reading about them. Rather, we need to visually absorb the process.

In a particularly illuminating essay called *A Good Farmer of the Old School*, Berry recounts a series of conversations with an old friend and dairy farmer, Lancie Clippinger. Lancie writes of how, ironically, he has financially profited more by keeping the number of the cows he owns to a manageable number—specifically, to the number that he can see at one time. "If a fellow milks twenty-five cows," says Lancie, "he'll see them all."[35] When there are more, various problems occur. In another essay on wilderness, he expands on this theme of seeing natural processes: "Breeders of domestic animals, likewise, know that, when a breeding program is too much governed by human intention, by economic considerations, or by fashion, uselessness is the result. Size or productivity, for instance, will be gained at the cost of health, vigor, or reproductive ability."[36]

The moral, then, is that by getting visual access to nature's processes, we will be in a better position to see how the mechanistic consensus is metaphysically spurious, and more importantly, why nature's norms should shape our own. Consider what Aristotle says about the importance of habituation. In order to be proper members of our kind, we have to be properly formed, and this formation cannot entirely happen from within. Indeed, we should assume, correctly, that our formation will come through others. Stanley Hauerwas words the point rather strongly: "I can think of no more conformist message in liberal societies than the idea that students should learn to think for themselves. What must be said is that most students in our society do not have minds well enough trained to think. A central pedagogical task is to tell students that their problem is that they do not have minds worth making up. That is why training is so important, because training involves the formation of the self through submission to authority that will provide people with the virtues necessary to make reasoned judgment."[37] With this in mind, we might ask two questions. First—might a correct epistemic access to reality require not just correct teaching and the correct emulation of *virtuous* people, but also some direct and sustained access to nature itself? Secondly, does our industrial life *encourage* the banal motto "think for yourself"?

When one sees nature only through one's laptop screensaver, and when the ebb and flow of the seasons are incidental to one's workday—indeed, when one thinks nothing of buying fresh blueberries in January and sees only the final store-ready version of our daily bread—it is easy to understand, regardless of education or income, why traditional natural law has become passé. Our technological environments tailor us to the mechanistic consensus. We simply do not see nature as enchanted or *mysterious*, let alone *normative*, anymore, even as we might still find it *beautiful*. But beauty is in the eye of the beholder. Our industrial environments led us toward biological dualism, and it is this dualism—with its mechanical nature on one hand, and its autonomous mental agents on the other—that largely shapes our modern moral outlook, that (on the one hand) reduces material nature to Newtonian bits, and (on the other hand) encourages us to "think for ourselves," or at best, to study only moral theories that take practical reason as *sui generis*. As a result, we often live in opposition to nature and have suffered the natural consequences of this alienation. Wendell Berry's writing can therefore be seen as part of an antidote to our current industrial predicament: "I am only pointing out, as many others have done, that, by living in opposition to nature, we can cause natural calamities of which we would otherwise be free."[38] While an optimistic prognosis to our current state is not forthcoming, we might at the very least provide some pushback against our industrialized epistemic alienation by listening to the pleadings of Wendell Berry.

Notes

1. I use the label "traditional" in order to distinguish the version of natural law that I endorse (as well as the sort that Berry's writing can help illuminate) from what is sometimes called "new" natural law. My intention is not to belabor at length the points of distinction, important as they are, but merely to note by the "traditional" label that there is indeed a distinction to be made. In particular, traditional natural law, as opposed to new natural law, does not see any power in the celebrated naturalistic fallacy argument, precisely because traditional natural law is happy to see in the myriad substances in nature all of the immanent aims and ends that are really there, and happy to take from these substances all that they give, demand, and proscribe. Traditional natural law theorists are explicit in their reliance on the powers of (material) natural substances apart from mere (immaterial) "rationality" to manifest immanent oughts, whereas "new" natural law is content to derive human norms from what it sees as the special features of our practical reason alone. So, for example, the traditional natural law theorist will, and the new natural law theorist will not, see power in the "perverted faculty argument," which argues for the

wrong of contraception not just because it is not properly or "completely" "self-giving," but more basically because it is contrary to the normative ends of our sundry biological faculties. See especially the second section of Edward Feser's essay, "In Defense of the Perverted Faculty Argument" (Edward Feser, *Neo-Scholastic Essays* (South Bend, IN: St. Augustine's Press, 2015), 379-387) for an extended discussion of the differences between traditional and new natural law theory.
2. James Barham, "The Emergence of Biological Value," in *Debating Design: From Darwin to DNA*, ed. William Dembski and Michael Ruse (Cambridge: Cambridge University Press, 2004) 210ff.
3. Jacob Hoeger, "Missing the Night Sky." *The New Atlantis: A Journal of Technology and Society,* 48(2016) 115-131.
4. Cf. Mark Mitchel and Nathan Schlueter, ed. *The Humane Vision of Wendell Berry* (Wilmington, DE: ISI Books, 2011) and Joel James Shuman and Roger Owen, ed. *Wendell Berry and Religion: Heaven's Earthly Life* (Clark Lectures) (Lexington, KY: The University Press of Kentucky, 2009).
5. Magazines that have carried Berry's essays and interviews include *Dissent, The Nation, The Progressive, Orion,* and even *Playboy*. Suffice it to say, these are not publications where one can find a passionate defense of conservative positions on the meaning of sex and the family.
6. Philippa Foot, *Natural Goodness* (New York: Oxford University Press, 2001), especially chapters 2 and 3.
7. Cf. Alasdair MacIntyre, *Dependent Rational Animals* (Peru, IL: Carus Publishing Company, 2001) 21ff.
8. Michael Thompson, "The Representation of Life," in *Virtues and Reasons: Philippa Foot and Moral Theory* ed. Rosalind Hursthouse et al. (Oxford: Clarenden Press, 1995).
9. Conor Cunningham, *Darwin's Pious Idea* (Grand Rapids, MI: Eerdmans Publishing, 2010) 184.
10. Hans Jonas, *The Phenomenon of Life* (Evanston: Northwestern University Press, 2001), 57.
11. Wendell Berry, "Getting Along with Nature," in *Home Economics*, Wendell Berry (San Francisco: North Point Press, 1987), 15.
12. William Ophuls, *Plato's Revenge* (MIT Press, 2011).
13. Wendell Berry, "Six Agricultural Fallacies," in *Home Economics*, 123.
14. Rupert Sheldrake, *Science Set Free* (New York: Deepak Chopra Books, 2013), 48.
15. James Barham, "The Emergence of Biological Value," 212.
16. Michael Sandel, *Justice: What's the Right Thing to Do?* (New York: Farrar, Straus, and Giroux, 2009), 189.
17. Richard Louv, *Last Child in the Woods: Saving Our Children From Nature-Deficit Disorder* (Algonquin Books, 2008), 2.

18. David Oderberg, "Teleology: Organic and Inorganic," in *Contemporary Perspectives on Natural Law: Natural Law as a Limiting Concept*, Ana Marta Gonzalez, ed. (New York: Routledge, 2008) 260.
19. See chapter 10 of Peter Simpson's *Political Illiberalism* (Transaction Publishers, 2015), 211ff for a brilliant explanation of the *becoming* of embryonic development.
20. Rupert Sheldrake, *Science Set Free*, 44.
21. James Barham, "The Reality of Purpose and the Reform of Naturalism," *Philosophia Naturalis* 44:31:52, 2007, 36.
22. John Searle, *Minds, Brains, and Science* (Cambridge: Harvard University Press, 1984), ch. 2.
23. Wendell Berry, "Six Agricultural Fallacies," 123.
24. Wendell Berry, "Two Economies," in *The Art of Commonplace*, Norman Wirzba, ed. (Berkeley, CA: Counterpoint Press, 2002) 225.
25. Wendell Berry, "Two Economies," in *The Art of Commonplace*, 230.
26. Wendell Berry, "A Native Hill," in *The Art of Commonplace*, 25.
27. Wendell Berry, "Preserving Wildness," in *Home Economics*, 143.
28. Wendell Berry, "Getting Along with Nature," 15.
29. Wendell Berry, "Letter to Wes Jackson," 7.
30. Wendell Berry, "Two Economies," 230.
31. Steve Talbott, "A Conversation with Nature," 40.
32. Wendell Berry, "Letter to Wes Jackson," 6.
33. William Ophuls, *Plato's Revenge*, 45.
34. Wendell Berry, "Higher Education and Home Defense," in *Home Economics*, 50.
35. Wendell Berry, "A Good Farmer of the Old School," in *Home Economics*, 154.
36. Wendell Berry, "Preserving Wildness," 140.
37. Stanley Hauerwas, "Discipleship as a Craft, Church as a Disciplined Community," *The Christian Century*, 108 (27), 882.
38. Wendell Berry, "Two Economies," 232.

An Exploration of the Role of Inclination in the Promulgation of the Natural Law

James M. Jacobs

Introduction

There appears to be a paradox at the heart of natural law theory: the natural law claims to be a universal ethic, yet many people fail to act in accordance with it. This observation acknowledges two truths about natural law, one theoretical, the other practical. Theoretically, if natural law is to be a meaningful theory of ethics, its precepts must be evident to *all* people. If the precepts of the natural law are not evident, then there is no way natural law can claim to be a universal rational ethic. But this must be balanced by the practical point, the obvious empirical fact that the precepts of the natural law are widely flouted by apparently rational people. This would appear to undermine the theoretical claim.

In order to resolve this apparent paradox, defenders of the natural law have to demonstrate how the natural law, while known by all people, is not attended to by all. That it is known by all is an essential aspect of the tradition which insists that the natural law is evident by virtue of man's rationality. Indeed, Thomas Aquinas says quite directly that "the natural law is promulgated by the very fact that God instilled it into man's mind so as to be known by him naturally."[1] Yet the empirical fact of people acting in contradiction to the natural law also means that natural law theorists must offer a reasonable explanation for how that promulgation of the precepts of the natural law can be impeded. This would explain why people often behave in unnatural and irrational ways despite the universal nature of the promulgation.

Thomas and the natural law tradition, of course, suggest certain explanations for how the natural law may be "blotted out" from the hearts of men, especially in the secondary and tertiary precepts.[2] He mentions specifically how "reason is perverted by passion, or evil habit, or an evil disposition of nature;"[3] again, he will say that "vicious customs and corrupt habits"[4] lead men to embrace even unnatural vices. These conditions seem to explain individuals who are evil in particular circumstances or are vicious by habit.

The widespread moral turpitude of contemporary society raises a more fundamental question.[5] How might we explain more systematic inattention to natural law, where an entire society falls away from goodness?[6] In this paper, I would like to explore how a society as a whole might become deaf to the promulgation of even the first principles of natural law so as to distort moral judgment in a near universal fashion. The first principles of the natural law are those that follow most directly and universally from man's rational nature: man's temporal end is to live in society for the perfection of intellect and will, which in turn enables him to achieve his eternal end of knowing and loving God.[7] (These first principles follow analytically from the generic principle that good is to be done and evil is to be avoided.[8]) As first principles, these are understood to be the self-evident ends that inform all other actions which are chosen as means. As Thomas says, "The first principle in practical matters, which are the object of the practical reason, is the last end: and the last end of human life is bliss or happiness."[9] Happiness can be realized only by communion with other persons, human and divine; we are therefore naturally ordered to that communion. All specific acts are chosen as means to this end.[10] This position, however, intensifies the paradox stated above, for these self-evident and universal ends can never be blotted out from rational consideration. As self-evident first principles, they must remain the ultimate motivating goal of every human decision. How, then, can we act contrary to them?

What I would like to consider in this paper is that even if these ends cannot be blotted out, it might be possible that their significance be systematically distorted, so as to explain the moral decay of an entire society. My argument is that, in addition to personal vice, there are *cultural conditions* which can obscure the promulgation of the first principles of the natural law for an entire society. Culture enframes a people, constituting an often unrecognized prism through which a particular set of assumptions flourishes. As a result, a society's assumptions about metaphysics and anthropology, if mistaken, can impede the reception of natural law. Alasdair MacIntyre argues this point in his most recent book. There are, he says, "two important sources of practical error. One arises from the danger that we all confront of being led astray by our feelings and affections.... The other arises from the sometimes distorting and misleading influences of our own social and cultural order on our beliefs."[11] Culture can distort the promulgation of the natural law if it systemically distorts the nature of personal communion necessary for happiness. With respect especially to the first principles, we must insist that the natural law is still in the heart, we are still ordered to perfective relationships; it is only that their import is now misunderstood.

The crucial premise for my argument about how the first principles can be misunderstood is that the rational formulation of the precepts of the natural law—the usual locus of discussion with respect to natural law—is not man's original knowledge of the natural law. Rather, that formulation is a second order reflection upon man's inclinations by which the natural law is first known. I contend that these inclinations are themselves shaped by societal presuppositions.[12] Therefore, when these inclinations are perverted, then the second order reflection will either be wrong itself, or appear irrelevant because its truth is discordant with the experience of people. This would lead to widespread misunderstandings of the natural law, not only in theory but also in practice, such as we see today. Drawing on G.J. McAleer's argument that natural law orders man to ecstatic union, as well as MacIntyre's argument that natural law is intrinsically social, I will argue that the subjective turn in modern thought has distorted the meaning of love and interpersonal communion. Traditionally, love was seen as an ecstatic drive seeking union with a higher good; for moderns, love has become a self-regarding concern with the satisfaction of the subject. This condition of disordered love confounds our connatural knowledge of the natural law, and so makes it impossible to understand the proper ends of human action. In other words, I argue that it is the affective constitution of contemporary society which prevents us from grasping the truth of the natural law.[13]

The Promulgation of the Natural Law in Thomas Aquinas

Before considering how the knowledge of the natural law can be distorted, we first need to review what the natural law is and how it is promulgated in the normal case. In general, law is an "extrinsic principle moving us to good."[14] That law is an extrinsic principle implies that there are, prior to law, intrinsic principles by which man is moved to the good. The most basic intrinsic principle is the natural activity that flows from the form, for that activity is the perfection of the form: "All things created would seem, in a way, to be purposeless, if they lacked an operation proper to them; since the purpose of everything is its operation. For the less perfect is always for the sake of the more perfect: and consequently…the form which is the first act, is for the sake of its operation, which is the second act."[15] The good is nothing other than this perfection of the nature of the substance in activity.[16] There is, then, a natural dynamism in every form: the act of existence that constitutes the first act is naturally effusive in generating its second act, "for whatever does not yet participate in the act of being tends toward it by a certain natural appetite."[17] This second act, then, is the normative state of being for a nature. As Heinrich Rommen pithily notes, because the act of existence underlies both the stability of a nature's essence and the dynamism of the essence to its end, the ontological and the deontological orders are ultimately one.[18]

These acts are the result of natural inclinations to perfection or goodness manifested in the appetites.[19] As an attraction to the good, these appetites can also be called loves.[20] Although there are natural appetites that follow from any substantial form inasmuch as it is inclined to action, forms that possess knowledge are more perfect and so have appetite in a more perfect way. This higher appetitive inclination is elicited by awareness of a suitable object;[21] that is, the natural dynamism of the substance is directed to a specific object attendant upon cognition. Thus, man has appetites following upon both sensation, for particular goods, and intellection, for the universal good, or happiness.[22] However, since the will is inclined indifferently to the multitude of particular goods, and since the sensitive appetites are accompanied by passionate reactions which may impede good judgment,[23] these loves need some assistance to be properly directed. An intrinsic aid is virtue;[24] the extrinsic aid is law. Thus, law exists to assist us in evaluating the potential goods presented to us, especially in the absence of virtue.[25]

I review these basics because this illuminates the problems concerning the promulgation of the natural law. As extrinsic, the natural law needs to be made known to man. Thomas insists that "in order that a law obtain the binding force which is proper to a law, it must needs be applied to the men who have to be ruled by it. Such application is made by its being notified to them by promulgation."[26] Since the natural law must be promulgated to all who are measured by it, that promulgation must be made to all humans, or else we cannot properly call it a law.

The relevance of this idea of universal promulgation becomes clear when we consider Thomas's definition of the natural law:

> Since all things subject to Divine providence are ruled and measured by the eternal law…it is evident that all things partake somewhat of the eternal law, in so far as, namely, from its being imprinted on them, they derive their respective inclinations to their proper acts and ends. Now among all others, the rational creature is subject to Divine providence in the most excellent way, in so far as it partakes of a share of providence, by being provident both for itself and for others. Wherefore it has a share of the Eternal Reason, whereby it has a natural inclination to its proper act and end: and this participation of the eternal law in the rational creature is called the natural law.[27]

This definition of natural law incorporates both the intrinsic and extrinsic principles moving man to perfection. First, the appetite of creatures for the good operates with law-like necessity because it is a manifestation of the eternal law through which God creates the universe, giving creatures their forms, appetites, and activities.[28] Thomas equates this plan of divine reason with the providential order of Creation: "In created things good is found not only as regards their substance, but also as regards their order towards an end and especially their last end…. Since, however, God is the cause of things by His intellect…it is necessary that the type of the order of things towards their end should pre-exist in the divine mind: and the type of things ordered towards an end is, properly speaking, providence."[29] That same providential order of creation, when considered as in the mind of God, is the eternal law, for "the eternal law is nothing else than the type of Divine Wisdom, as directing all actions and movements."[30] Thus, all creatures are inclined to action according to the eternal law; for this reason, we can say that the eternal law is made manifest in the appetites of creatures.[31]

It is the regularity of these appetitive inclinations that enables man to know the *eternal* law. But it is also by rationally reflecting on his own appetitive inclinations that man knows the *natural* law, for that knowledge would demand that he act in accord with the eternal law. As Thomas strikingly says, man can abet the created order by acting *providentially* for himself and others. In other words, the natural law is a rational awareness of those patterns of behavior necessary for perfection which inform action so that a person might fulfill his divinely given vocation.

It is clear, then, that knowledge of the natural law must arise from the inclinations which reveal the providential order of the eternal law. Thomas says this explicitly in elucidating the precepts of the natural law: "Since…good has the nature of an end, and evil, the nature of a contrary, hence it is that all those things to which man has a natural inclination, are naturally apprehended by reason as being good, and consequently as objects of pursuit, and their contraries as evil, and objects of avoidance. Wherefore according to the order of natural inclinations, is the order of the precepts of the natural law."[32] These inclinations are essential to the promulgation of the natural law because "God imprints on the whole of nature the principles of its proper actions" and so "the impression of an inward active principle is to natural things, what the promulgation of law is to men."[33] This inclination to activity is that whereby God makes known what actions a nature ought to pursue.

Again, though, in man this impression to action takes on a twofold significance, for it not only moves him to act, it also provides evidence for conceptualizing that end in terms of a rational formulation of the natural law. As Thomas says, "Since the rational nature, together with that which it has in common with all creatures, has something proper to itself inasmuch as it is rational, consequently it is subject to the eternal law in both ways; because while each rational creature has some knowledge of the eternal law…it also has a natural inclination to that which is in harmony with the eternal law."[34] Through the eternal law, man is inclined by his appetites to his end; through reason, he conceptualizes this inclination in terms of the precepts of the natural law. This explains how the natural imperative of the inclinations becomes a moral imperative: man by reason can know this ordering to the good, and so has a responsibility to act in accord with it.[35]

The promulgation of the natural law, then, implies a collaboration of appetite and intellect. As Denis Bradley notes, "In the Thomistic schema, the natural inclinations of the will and the innate intellectual habit of synderesis, not acquired moral virtue, are the foundations of moral reasoning. In itself, the will has a natural inclination to certain basic ends that is prior to any intellectual grasp of these ends."[36] The appetite orders man to the good by nature, and in so doing makes evident the laws of nature; the intellect, ordered to truth, properly interprets those inclinations to perfective activity and discerns the precepts of the natural law which guide the will in the pursuit of perfection. This is why the precepts of the natural law cannot be abstract deontological rules about basic goods, but must be known by reflection on appetitive inclinations or loves: "Every act of reason and will in us is based on that which is according to nature…for every act of reasoning is based on principles that are known naturally, and every act of appetite in respect of the means is derived from the natural appetite in respect of the last end. Accordingly the first direction of our acts to their end must needs be in virtue of the natural law."[37] As Thomas notes elsewhere, "nature comes before intellect,"[38] so that the natural dynamism or inclination of the will to the good in general is prior to any cognition of our nature.[39] The will is itself an orientation to happiness as final cause, and this is necessarily prior to any specification of choice to a particular good.[40] That is, it is inclinations as known by reason that reveal the natural law to us.

Some might object at this point that my emphasis on the appetites is inappropriate, for Thomas makes it clear that the natural law—all law—is an act of reason.[41] To this objection, I would make three replies. First, as already argued, I would reiterate the importance of man's two-fold participation in the eternal law. The eternal law is an act of Divine practical reason that manifests itself in our appetites, which are then reflected on by reason in the formulation of the precepts of the natural law. Second, I would argue that the will, as the rational appetite, naturally orders us to what is in accord with human dignity as rational. This makes possible non-reflective judgments as a basis for a connatural knowledge of the natural law. Third, I would suggest that the emphasis on love is a retrieval of the Augustinian contribution to the natural law tradition. This strain salubriously combines with Aristotelian intellectualism to present a more complete picture of human action. Let us now consider these latter two points.

The Connatural Knowledge of the Natural Law

We see at this point why the rational formulation of the natural law—the precepts and rules—are a second order reflection on the inclinations. Indeed, the original knowledge of natural law arises unreflectively with those inclinations because it is a connatural knowledge. Connatural knowledge is the non-conceptual receptivity to being in terms of truth and goodness that enables man to know a truth, even in the absence of conceptual knowledge.

Thomas introduces the idea of connatural knowledge by noting, "Rectitude of judgment is twofold: first, on account of perfect use of reason, secondly, on account of a certain connaturality with the matter about which one has to judge."[42] Rational judgments are made on the basis of antecedent cognitions, which ultimately refer back to self-evident principles. This is how the precepts of the natural law direct action. But, as Yves Simon ruefully comments, "It would be very unfortunate if this were the only way of judgment."[43] For in addition to these purely rational judgments are judgments made on the basis of inclination. In fact, Simon argues that the "natural law is known by way of inclination before it is known by way of cognition."[44] This is because our natural appetites find goods attractive and evils repellant. The natural law is originally known in those well-ordered inclinations to the good as that which is consonant with human nature. Similarly, Jacques Maritain notes that connatural knowledge is what distinguishes the virtuous man from the moral philosopher—who all too often is a rogue.[45] He says, "The genuine concept of Natural Law is the concept of a law which is natural not only insofar as it expresses the normality of functioning of human nature, but also insofar as it is *naturally known*, that is, known through inclination or through connaturality, not through conceptual knowledge and by way of reasoning."[46] Humankind knows the natural law before any professor steps to the podium; this is because it is a connatural knowledge derived from our inclinations, especially of the will's order to happiness as found in communion with others.

Now, this connatural knowledge does not excuse us from the work of making rational judgments, for we can only accept the verdict of inclination if those inclinations are sound. We ascertain soundness by reflecting on inclinations in light of the speculative knowledge of human nature and its operative perfections which is the premise for practical reason.[47] These rational reflections not only give justification to our inclinations, but they also make them communicable in terms of universal judgments, that is, laws. This then grounds a secondary mode of connatural knowledge, that of virtue.[48] This second order reflection, then, is crucial for the moral life of society, but it is nevertheless second order.

We noted that the judgment will be sound only if inclinations are sound. However, it follows that if our inclinations are corrupt, we cannot trust the connatural knowledge that arises from them. In fact, as Simon points out, to try to formulate precepts in abstraction from this connatural knowledge of the good, "when judgment by inclination is completely gone…when freedom from tradition is recklessly asserted," can only lead to illusions and empty rationalizations.[49] We *could* undertake the purely theoretical project of constructing the precepts of the natural law by an abstract analysis of human nature as the objective standard for action. But without the proper connatural knowledge, this would lack the affective immediacy a moral theory ought to have,[50] and so would strike people as irrelevant and arbitrary commandments.[51]

If our knowledge of the natural law is first known through our inclinations, any alteration in our inclinations would affect the connatural knowledge that arises from them, and so seriously obscure the natural law for an entire society.[52] In fact, society can function *only* when most people implicitly approve of that connatural knowledge of natural law, even if they vociferously object to the theory as formulated in reflection, for only then are they ordered to the true good.[53] But the opposite case—moral theorizing in the absence of connaturality—can only lead to individual disaster and social disintegration.

Natural Law and Love in Augustine

In addition to this non-conceptual connatural knowledge, we also note that acknowledging the centrality of love is recovering Augustine's contribution to the tradition. While the Greek tradition emphasized the cognitive reflection on human nature as the source of natural law, Augustine will be the first to fully appreciate the volitional source of natural law.[54] For Augustine, the moral law is embodied in a correct ordering of loves; moreover, that love is the foundation of society. Thus, a society with disordered love can only be one in which the natural law is obscured.

Augustine defines wisdom in terms not of cognition, but of appetite: it is "nothing other than the truth in which the highest good is discerned and acquired."[55] This highest good can be attained only if it is loved more than anything else. Consequently, evil is defined as inordinate desire,[56] that is, loving those things which, not being eternal, can be lost against one's will.[57] This is why the correct order of love is wisdom: Augustine reserves "the term 'wise' for those whom truth demands should be called wise, those who have achieved peace by placing all inordinate desire under the control of the mind."[58] And yet, this peace, a "tranquility of order,"[59] also extends to society as a whole, reflecting its ordinate love. Augustine famously defines a people as "an assemblage of reasonable beings bound together by a common agreement as to the objects of their love. [Therefore,] in order to discover the character of any people, we have only to observe what they love."[60] Based on this, he asserts that there are really only two kinds of society: "The one consists of those who wish to live after the flesh, the other of those who wish to live after the spirit."[61] Only when people love ordinately—loving God and man above all else—can there be a lasting peace, for true community emerges spontaneously in mutual love of the highest good.[62] This idea of love as pulling man toward society and toward God—toward the highest good—is fundamental to the later natural law tradition, for these are the primary precepts of Thomistic natural law as revealed by our natural inclinations.

The Optimism of Thomistic Natural Law

The Thomistic understanding of natural law is based upon an optimistic view of human nature as oriented to fulfillment in a transcendent good. This requires that man be able to go beyond the blinkered selfishness of his own subjectivity. G. J. McAleer convincingly demonstrates that this ecstatic desire is foundational to natural law in his *Ecstatic Morality and Sexual Politics*.[63] The natural tendency toward ecstasy is evidenced in the fact that in moving up the hierarchy of appetites—natural, sensitive, rational[64]—man seeks a broader realization of the good: "The least ecstatic desire converts its object into itself while the most ecstatic desire is converted into its object."[65] He begins by noting, "Thomas describes a metaphysical order which in ascending in perfection becomes increasingly ecstatic as the more perfect members of the order find their proper good in sustaining, protecting, and promoting other members of the order that are increasingly remote from themselves."[66] This metaphysical order is reflected in inclinations of man which are the foundation for the natural law: there is first the natural inclination of all beings to preserve themselves; then, there is the inclination of animals to reproduce the species; finally, there are the peculiarly rational inclinations that lead man to live in society and to know God.[67] McAleer sees in this an ever-greater circle of extroverted activity: "The metaphysical order of ecstatic being—individual-conservation, species-offspring, genus-community, universal-God—is expressed in human desire. Human appetite is a set of ordered movements from conservation (individual), to family (species), to civic life (genus), and to God (universal)."[68] This tendency to ecstasy shows that at the heart of all our desires is an *eros*: a desire for fulfillment in union with others.[69] There is, in this eroticism, a fundamental openness to the being and goodness of others, of the cosmos, and especially of God Himself.[70]

    Therefore, the inclinations of human nature, in seeking ecstatic union, aim to complete the potentiality of man by giving the self to the other. The ends of man lie in the social intercourse by which he perfects his capacity for wisdom and love, which in turn leads him to a knowledge of and union with God. But the actualizations commanded in natural law are possible only if we decenter the self. Indeed, we might say that the principle of self-preservation is justified only as a condition for becoming part of a "we" that is greater that the self: a species, a political society, or the Communion of Saints. In self-preservation, I assimilate the other to me; yet this self-preservation ultimately can only be justified in converting myself to the other through ecstatic union.[71] In other words, we exist to be of service to neighbor and God, because in that service we find fulfillment of our potentiality.

Obscuring Connaturality by Distorting Love

The natural law, then, urges man to be ecstatic, to live in a well-ordered society for the common good and to seek union with God. These are the appetites that follow upon the will as rational: to love the other by finding union with them. These inclinations make man not primarily self-regarding, but other-regarding. McAleer contrasts these alternatives: "Human nature has two possibilities: either sensuality is obedient to reason and the person lives ecstatically in service of the other, or sensuality is unresponsive to reason and the person is reduced to self-concern."[72] That is, if we fail to recognize the tendency to ecstasy, we turn in and focus only on that self-regarding desire. The will must still drive us to love God and neighbor, but instead of giving ourselves over to them—opening ourselves to be enriched by the other—we instead admit them only insofar as they can be converted to our purposes. Our love of the other is for the sake of the self; because it is reduced, it fails to enrich and perfect. It is this distortion of love that will inevitably debase our connatural knowledge of the natural law.

Alasdair MacIntyre suggests modernity as a whole makes the error of giving primacy to these self-regarding desires. In *Ethics in the Conflicts of Modernity*, MacIntyre presents a detailed analysis of the relationship between desire and moral reasoning. His premise is that there are only two options: an objective standard for good based on Aristotelianism or an ultimately subjective idea of good based on emotivism (or expressivism). Against the modern expressivist position, which sees the ultimate end as an object of personal desire, he argues for the Aristotelian position that sees that objective flourishing can only be conceived of and attained in a social context. Given this social nature of morality, he describes the natural law as "that law whose authority we need to recognize in virtue of our nature as rational agents, [whose precepts] are needed to structure the relationships of those who pursue their individual and common good in the company of others."[73] This is necessary both because we learn from others, whose wisdom helps to objectify our desires, but also because man's good is itself a social good,[74] one attained only in cooperative acts which make possible the development of virtue, love, and wisdom. As MacIntyre says, "those relationships require a high degree of mutual trust, that it is a fact that without those relationships human powers cannot be fully developed."[75] Though he does not state it in this way, we can see that he too is insisting on the ecstatic nature of the human good in community.[76]

    MacIntyre's argument focuses on practical reasoning and cognition of the criteria of the good. I, however, would argue that his analysis can be extended to the desires themselves, for disordered love would undermine the requisite trust and civic amity needed for happiness. It is precisely with respect to love that expressivism is so destructive. Its good is defined in terms of subjective, self-referential desire. It is an atomism that kills the tendency to ecstatic union, and thereby impairs the connatural knowledge of the natural law. Where the natural law's good has an objective standard of flourishing which can only be attained in ecstatic union with others, the expressivist, by contrast, only judges society in terms of the satisfaction of an individual's preferences, which are the products of subjective intuition alone. Instead of a person evaluating himself in terms of the community's good, the community is assessed through its ability to satisfy the individual. As MacIntyre comments, "What the social context provides is a setting for *her* actions and reactions. What the history of her relationships provides is insight into aspects of *her* history."[77] There is no referent to shared flourishing, because the possibility of ecstatic union has been cut off. Love is reduced to satisfaction of the self.

    McAleer had made the point that while the first inclination for self-preservation converts the other to the self, the higher, ecstatic inclinations converts the self to others. In MacIntyre's analysis of expressivism, there is no impulse to go beyond the self and realize the ecstatic inclinations. Ecstasy is rendered impossible in modernity.[78] As a result, the only desires that remain are those that seek to reduce the other to his or her usefulness for the subject. I am interested in my neighbor and God only insofar as they are of service to me; if they are not, I am entitled to ignore them. In other words, love is reduced to concupiscence, where individual benefit is the sole criterion, and the objective good—the natural law itself—can no longer be discovered in the inclinations.[79]

Modernity and the Loss of Ecstatic Eros

MacIntyre decries the grotesque condition in which modern morality finds itself. Something has turned our inclinations away from their natural erotic ecstasy to the self-regarding notion in which love of self has primacy. This devolution is evident in the transformation of the notion of natural law itself in modernity from an ecstatic communion in terms of just relations to a focus on the egocentric claims of natural right.[80] Where for Thomas the natural law was ecstatically ordered to union with God and neighbor as the greatest good (*summum bonum*), modern natural law in Hobbes and Locke reflect the primacy of self-regard and fear of the other in that its precepts aim at the avoidance of the greatest evil (*summum malum*).[81] Now, I conclude this exploration by offering an admittedly tentative explanation for this epochal transformation of the nature of love.

My suggestion is that this is a result of the turn to the subject in modernity. The consequences of this for epistemology have long been recognized, from Descartes's *cogito* to Kant's Copernican Revolution. But I believe this turn to the subject causes degeneracy in love by making the self the primary and final reference of desire. There is a parallel introversion occurring: just as the mind is no longer turned outward to receive the truth, so the will is no longer turned outward to discover the good in the *existence* of other things. Because of cultural conditions which continually reaffirm this, like the individualism of Protestant religion[82] (Jesus is my personal savior) and the egalitarianism of democracy[83] (all opinions are equally valid), the good is sought only in that which is pleasing or useful for the subject himself. Human nature still inclines us to the entire hierarchy of appetites, but the occlusion of the ecstatic goal will inevitably distort the connatural knowledge that is the basis of the natural law.[84]

Indeed, the ecstatic drive is now an occasion for fear: assuming others are equally self-regarding, the neighbor is seen as one demanding recognition in terms of rights, and God is seen as one demanding recognition in terms of worship. Neither relation is seen as integral to human happiness. In this way, the promulgation of the natural law is corrupted by the inordinate desires, the disordered loves, of our cultural context which inculcates the idea that the other is for the sake of the self, as opposed to the self as being for the sake of the other. Matthew Levering nicely captures how the idea of natural law is corrupted: "[Most] modern thinkers...[conceive] of human nature as self-contained rather than ordered beyond itself, and so [their] 'natural law' will pertain to the fulfillment of the individual rather than to a set of relationships in which human beings find their fulfillment as members of a society or as guided toward 'ecstatic' fulfillment by an ordering established by God."[85] There is possibly no better evidence of this than the collapse of fertility rates in the West;[86] that most ecstatic expression of love, the marital act ordered to childbirth, has given way to empty sensuality.

Accordingly, one of the clearest illustrations of the degeneration of our love that emerges from the turn to the subject is how the erotic itself has come to be seen. From Plato to Aquinas, the erotic was a draw from the temporal to the transcendent, from the introverted to the ecstatic; for moderns, the erotic has been debased to the merely romantic, or worse, the pornographic. In some sense, it remains the sum of all desires, but the type of satisfaction it promises has utterly changed. As a guide to this denigration of the erotic, let us consider the diagnosis of the late Italian philosopher, Augusto Del Noce, in the book *The Crisis of Modernity*.[87]

Del Noce sees the source of modernity's problems in a rejection of any need for transcendence in favor of wholly immanent relations. This begins with a rejection of God, a metaphysical rebellion which becomes a moral rebellion obliterating ethics because it is a "refusal to respect being and to be faithful to objective norms."[88] Absent the transcendent, all that remains is a purely horizontal causality, a worldview epitomized by scientism, secularism, and purely sexual eroticism. A purely mundane world is ultimately one in which the only criterion for value is desire alone. Since there is no higher causality to justify these desires, expression of these desires becomes a sheer assertion of power.[89] This means that scientism, secularism, and eroticism naturally tend to totalitarianism, where unjustifiable values are maintained only by the suppression of dissenting opinion.[90] Del Noce describes how the sole foundation of value is this debased eroticism: "Having taken away every order of ends and eliminated every authority of values, all that is left is vital energy, which can be identified with sexuality.... Hence, the core element of life will be sexual happiness."[91] Paired with scientism, this is particularly problematic, for the only value that scientism can allow is biological, that is, sexual vitality; this so dominates that all inclination to the transcendent must be repudiated or reinterpreted. This reductionism then turns human nature against itself, for as Del Noce concludes, "In every totalitarian system, what starts as persecution of *religion* mutates into persecution of *reason*...which becomes negation of ethics when it is turned into an absolute."[92] The rejection of God, then, leads to the annihilation of man, for there is no way for him to realize the rational ends realized in communion. The turn to the subject turns *eros* toward the self, a condition which can never result in satisfaction; these desires, then, become more and more totalitarian due to the very futility of their pursuit.[93] We now see the fruit of this, where the most virulent attacks on the natural law come in the arena of sexual ethics, for it is there that the debased eroticism of modernity most resolutely refuses redirection to the ecstasy that characterizes the true way to happiness.[94]

This cultural corruption of *eros* is clearly very different from the way passions might affect one's ability to fulfill the nature law. Passions are momentary; while they can blot out the precepts of the natural law, their effect is ephemeral. Passion may be said to blind us; however, the impassioned man is, in the words of Robert

Spaemann, "responsible for his inability to see." Spaemann contrasts this with what he calls "dullness of spirit… [in which] an obtuse person perceives no hierarchy of values."[95] Our depraved *eros* has in fact led to this dullness of spirit. This is a more difficult moral problem to remedy. Any society which has lost its erotic orientation to ecstatic transcendence is one that is insensible to the goods we by nature seek. The inclinations of that society constantly misrepresent what man must do to fulfill the natural law. The result is a stupor of affective disease, for which a cure is obsessively but futilely sought. The futility of this desire is borne out in the anomie which characterizes modernity; one scholar catalogues the failure of self-regard in terms of "a whole range of [modernity's] uncertainties and pathologies, from Locke's sense of 'uneasiness,' Rousseau's '*amour-propre*,' Hegel's 'unhappy consciousness,' and Kierkegaard's 'anxiety' to Tocqueville's 'inquietude,' Marx's 'alienation,' and Weber's 'disenchantment.'"[96] This obsessive focus on the self and the debasement of eros clearly has not advanced the satisfaction of the appetite of man.

Conclusion

Modern society seems deaf to the promulgation of the natural law not because it is not in our hearts, nor because we are less rational; rather, it is because our appetites, the locus of the original promulgation of natural law, have been so distorted that we no longer understand what the inclination to happiness entails. Everyone acknowledges that love is the universal engine of human activity, but we no longer understand what love is. While St. Paul understood the moral seriousness that goes with professing "Love never fails,"[97] today the most unnatural vices are defended by invoking the empty dictum, "Love wins." Instead of focusing on fulfilling spiritual faculties in union with others, we seek only subjective satisfaction of ephemeral appetite.

Archbishop Charles Chaput has correctly diagnosed our situation as one in which eros is depraved: "The surest way to transform a culture is from the inside out. And the surest path to doing it isn't through reasoned debate (too tedious) or violence (too costly) but by colonizing and reshaping the culture's appetites and behaviors.... Modesty, virginity, celibacy, sexual restraint: These words are dust magnets in today's vocabulary, antibiotics past their expiration date."[98]

The natural law still teaches us to love, but that love has been disfigured by the modern Pharisees who do not even know the Law.

Notes

1. *Summa Theologica* I-II.90.4.ad 1. Citations from the translation by the Fathers of the English Dominican Province (New York: Benzinger, 1948). Henceforth *ST*.
2. *ST* I-II.94.6; parallel arguments are made in articles 4 and 5. Importantly, in all three articles, this ignorance of the natural law cannot extend to the primary precepts, for those are self-evident and so accessible to all men.
3. *ST* I-II.94.4. On passion as a cause of sin, see I-II.77.2.
4. *ST* I-II.94.6.
5. Thus, where John Courtney Murray confidently described the American regime in the 1950s as embodying the tradition of natural law, many thinkers today say that the Lockean foundation of America creates a society whose "unsustainable liberalism" is naturally corrosive of the moral order and of society itself. As a consequence of contemporary moral decline, there is great controversy concerning the place of natural law in the founding the America. For Murray, see *We Hold These Truths* (New York NY: Sheed and Ward, 1960), 1-43; for the latter opinion, see Patrick J. Deneen, "Unsustainable Liberalism" *First Things* 225 (August/September 2012), 25-31.
6. The proper theological answer is original sin (*ST* I-II.82.3). Yet Thomas is also clear that original sin does not deprave human nature itself (*ST* I-II.85.1), so political society can still be erected on strong moral foundations of natural law.
7. *ST* I-II.94.2.
8. On the distinction between primary, secondary, and tertiary principles of the natural law, including the relation of them to the principle that "the good is to be done and evil avoided," see James Jacobs, "The Precepts of the Decalogue and the Problem of Self-evidence," *International Philosophical Quarterly* 47.4 (Dec. 2007), 399-415.
9. *ST* I.90.2.
10. *ST* I.82.1, I.82.2, and I-II.13.3.
11. Alasdair MacIntyre, *Ethics in the Conflicts of Modernity: An Essay on Desire, Practical Reasoning, and Narrative* (Cambridge: Cambridge University Press, 2016), 75.

12. This also is an important part of MacIntyre's argument: "What desires agents have, how those desires are felt and expressed, and how they are related to the practical reasoning of agents vary both within and between social and culture orders" (*Ethics in the Conflicts of Modernity*, 120).
13. Charles Sanders Peirce argues that one's affective constitution can impede recognizing the existence of God. Knowledge of God is a natural result of the ability of the intellect to play with respect to ultimate causal explanations, but a pessimistic person refuses to entertain such logical abductions and so closes himself off from the truth. See "A Neglected Argument for the Reality of God," *Collected Papers of Charles Sanders Peirce*, ed. by Charles Hartshorne and Paul Weiss (Cambridge, MA: Harvard University Press, 1931), VI. para. 452-493. My argument seeks to expand on this insight.
14. *ST* I-II.90.proem. Grace is the other extrinsic principle by which man is moved to the good.
15. *ST* I.105.5. Cf. SCG III.113.1: "Each thing appears to exist for the sake of its operation; indeed, operation is the ultimate perfection of a thing." For an overview of this point, see W. Norris Clarke, SJ, "Action as the Self-Revelation of Being: A Central Theme in the Thought of St. Thomas" in *Explorations in Metaphysics: Being, God, Person* (Notre Dame, IN: University of Notre Dame Press, 1995), 45-64.
16. *ST* I.5.1.ad 1.
17. *De Veritate* 21.2.c.; see also *DV* 22.1.sc 4, and *SCG* III.16.3.
18. Heinrich Rommen, *The Natural Law: A Study in Legal and Social History and Philosophy*, trans. by Thomas R. Hanley, O.S.B. (Indianapolis: Liberty Fund, 1998), 143.
19. *ST* I.80.1.
20. *ST* I-II.26.1: "Now in each of these appetites, the name 'love' is given to the principle movement towards the end loved."
21. *ST* I.78.1.
22. *ST* I.82.1; cf. *SCG* II.47-48. Thomas argues that as ordered to the universal good, the will includes the pursuit of all particular goods (I-II.10.1): "Now this is good in general, to which the will tends naturally, as does each power to its object;... For it is not only things pertaining to the will that the will desires, but also that which pertains to each power, and to the entire man."
23. *ST* I.81.2 and I-II.22 and 23.
24. *ST* I-II.49.proem; cf. I-II.55.1: "Virtue denotes a certain perfection of a power. Now a thing's perfection is considered chiefly in regard to its end. But the end of power is act. Wherefore power is said to be perfect, according as it is determinate to its act."
25. *ST* I-II. 92.1.ad 1: "And since law is given for the purpose of directing human acts; as far as human acts conduce to virtue, so far does law make men good." Cf. *ST* I-II.94.3: "Since the rational soul is the proper form of man, there is

in every man a natural inclination to act according to reason: and this is to act according to virtue. Consequently, considered thus, all acts of virtue are prescribed by the natural law: since each one's reason naturally dictates to him to act virtuously."

26. *ST* I-II.90.1.
27. *ST* I-II.91.2.
28. The act of creation, for Thomas, has three elements: the production of creatures, the distinction between them, and the governance of the whole ordered to perfection; *ST* I.44.proem.
29. *ST* I.22.1.
30. *ST* I-II.93.1.
31. *ST* I-II.93.2: "A thing may be known in two ways: first, in itself; secondly, in its effect, wherein some likeness of that thing is found.... No one can know the eternal law, as it is in itself, except the blessed who see God in His Essence. But every rational creature knows it in its reflection, greater or less. For every knowledge of truth is a kind of reflection and participation of the eternal law, which is the unchangeable truth."
32. *ST* I-II.94.2.
33. *ST* I-II.93.5.c. and ad 1. Cf. *ST* I.103.8: "Every inclination of anything, whether natural or voluntary, is nothing but a kind of impression for the first mover; as the inclination of the arrow towards a fixed point is nothing but an impulse received from the archer. Wherefore every agent, whether natural or free, attains to its divinely appointed end, as though of its own accord."
34. *ST* I-II.93.6.
35. But, as noted earlier, this ordering of inclination and act is not infallible, because the sensitive appetites seek immediate satisfaction, and this may distort our evaluation of the goods at hand (*ST* I-II.77.2). It is for this reason that those who are disordered by passions and vices are subject to punishment (*ST* I-II.93.6).
36. Denis J.M. Bradley, *Aquinas on the Twofold Human Good: Reason and Human Happiness in Aquinas's Moral Science* (Washington, D.C.: The Catholic University of America Press, 1997), 245.
37. *ST* I-II.91.2.ad 2.
38. *ST* I.60.1. In *ST* I.82.4 and I-II *QQ*. 8-9, Thomas discusses the interaction of will and intellect. While it is clear that intellection must precede in the specification of a concrete moral act, it is nevertheless true that this choice is of the means to the end which the will desires by nature prior to consideration of any specification of means.
39. Thus, a human knows himself not first by some innate intuition, but only on reflection of the nature in act (*ST* I.87.1).
40. This natural dynamism is oriented to the good of perfection in general and is always operative as the foundation for human acts; Josef Pieper calls this

"simple willing" in *Living the Truth*, tr. by Stella Lange (San Francisco: Ignatius Press, 1989), 145-151, esp. at 146, and 179. Of course, even this simple willing presumes the general cognition of being, which is convertible with good and so is seen as perfective by the appetite in general; see *DV* 21.1.

41. *ST* I-II.90.1 and 94.1.
42. *ST* II-II.45.2; cf. *ST* I.1.6.ad 3.
43. Yves R. Simon, *The Tradition of Natural Law: A Philosopher's Reflection*, ed. by Vukan Kuic (New York: Fordham University Press, 1965), 127.
44. Simon, *Tradition of Natural Law*, 132.
45. Jacques Maritain, "On Knowledge through Connaturality" in *Natural Law: Reflections on Theory and Practice*, ed. William Sweet (South Bend, IN: St. Augustine's Press, 2001), 15. (This essay is also published in Maritain's *The Range of Reason* (New York: Scribner's, 1952), 22-29.)
46. Maritain, *Natural Law*, 20.
47. As Thomas succinctly asserts, "The speculative intellect by extension becomes practical" (*ST* I.79.11.sc). For a detailed elaboration of how practical reason is an extension of speculative reason, see Steven J. Jensen, *Knowing the Natural Law: From Precepts and Inclinations to Deriving Oughts* (Washington: The Catholic University of America Press, 2015).
48. The initial recourse to inclination should not be confused with this second, subsequent need for inclination, that of the judgment of prudence which applies the law, and is "the only way to ascertain practical judgments when that are considered concretely" (Simon, *Tradition of Natural Law*, 128).
49. Simon, *Tradition of Natural Law*, 136.
50. This is the fate of Enlightenment theories of natural law, which reflect not human nature but a priori deductions of rights, a procedure Ralph Barton Perry described as "credulous intuitionism" in *Puritanism and Democracy* (New York: Vanguard Press, 1944), 417.
51. This is the false vision of the Decalogue decried by John Paul II in *Veritatis Splendor*, nos. 35-53.
52. It might be objected that, as already noted, Thomas says, "The natural law is…instilled it into man's mind so as to be known by him naturally" (ST I-II.90.4.ad 1). Yet we must remember that no knowledge is innate for Thomas. What is "innate" is the prerational appetite for the good which motivates all human action, and the habit of synderesis by which this is understand rationally. Reason reflects on the appetites to ordain the precepts indicating the good.
53. Alasdair MacIntyre suggests such an argument in "How we can Learn what *Veritatis Splendor* has to Teach Us?" in *Veritatis Splendor and the Renewal of Moral Theology*, ed. by J. A. Dinoia, Avery Dulles, and Romanus Cessario (Downer's Grove, IL: Midwest Theological Forum, 1999), 73-94.
54. For a brief overview contrasting Cicero and Augustine, see Matthew Levering, *Biblical Natural Law: A Theocentric and Theological Approach* (Oxford: Oxford University Press, 2008), 71-82.

55. Augustine, *On Free Choice of the Will*, II.9, tr. by Thomas Williams (Indianapolis: Hackett, 1993).
56. Augustine, *On Free Choice*, I.3.
57. Augustine, *On Free Choice*, I.4. See also his distinction between those things that are loved for their use (uti), and those things which are to be loved for their own sake (*frui*) in *On Christian Doctrine*, Book I, esp. chapter 38.
58. Augustine, *On Free Choice*, I.9.
59. Augustine, *City of God*, XIX.13.
60. Augustine, *City of God*, XIX.24, tr. by Marcus Dods (New York: The Modern Library, 1950). This develops the argument of *On Free Choice*, I.14-16.
61. Augustine, *City of God*, XIV.1, cf. XIV.28.
62. Augustine, *City of God*, XIX.23.
63. G.J. McAleer, *Ecstatic Morality and Sexual Politics: A Catholic and Antitotalitarian Theory of the Body* (New York: Fordham University Press, 2005). His insightful argument relies particularly on two passages from *Summa Contra Gentiles*: III.24 and III.63.1-9.
64. Thomas discusses this hierarchy of appetite—natural, sensitive, and rational—in many places: e.g., *ST* I.59.1, I.80.1, and I-II.26.1.
65. McAleer, *Ecstatic Morality*, 19.
66. McAleer, *Ecstatic Morality*, 15.
67. *ST* I-II.94.2.
68. McAleer, *Ecstatic Morality*, 18.
69. Thomas Hibbs locates erotic desire as the driving force in human development: "An erotic pedagogy appeals to the ordered incompleteness of human nature, a sign of which is a longing for the good and the beautiful" (Hibbs, *Virtue's Splendor: Wisdom, Prudence and the Human Good* (New York: Fordham University Press, 2001), 173).
70. Therefore, as many have noted, in the natural law there is no conflict between *eros* and *agape*. See Josef Pieper, *Faith, Hope, Love*, tr. by Richard and Clara Winston (San Francisco: Ignatius Press, 1997), 185-241.
71. McAleer, *Ecstatic Morality*, 66. This is how McAleer frames the natural law: "The natural law is a participation in God according to Pseudo-Dionysius's *dictum bonum diffusivum sui est*.... The natural law of ecstatic being is a revelation of God."
72. McAleer, *Ecstatic Morality*, 75.
73. MacIntyre, *Ethics in the Conflicts of Modernity*, 57.
74. MacIntyre, *Ethics in the Conflicts of Modernity*, 51-52.
75. MacIntyre, *Ethics in the Conflicts of Modernity*, 60.
76. Natural law does not imply that an isolated individual can be self-correcting by knowing the natural law; rather, it implies that people together refine the pursuit of the various goods of man in accord with the highest goods represented in the common good. In addition to MacIntyre, see John Rist: *Real*

Ethics: Rethinking the Foundations of Morality (Cambridge: Cambridge University Press, 2002), 205-222.
77. MacIntyre, *Ethics in the Conflicts of Modernity*, 61; emphasis in original. See also 157-8, where MacIntyre asserts "she has been taught to think of herself in individualistic terms" by a market economy and the modern state. This position reminds us of Barack Obama's notorious "Life of Julia" campaign ad, in which an utterly solitary woman is born, attains maturity, gives birth, raises a child, and retires with no social relations whatsoever apart from the matriarchal oversight of the government.
78. Charles Taylor describes this as "the immanent frame" of modern secularism, in which the person is disengaged from all relations so as to be empowered to create his or her own values; see *A Secular Age* (Cambridge. MA: The Belknap Press of Harvard University Press, 2007), 539-593.
79. On the distinction between love as self-regarding concupiscence which seeks personal pleasure as opposed to the objective worth sought by benevolence, see *ST* I-II.27.3.
80. On this change, see the review of the arguments of Michel Villey by John Lamont, "In Defense of Villey on Objective Right" in *Truth and Faith in Ethics*, ed. by Hayden Ramsay (Charlottesville, VA: Imprint Academic, 2011), 177-198. For the historical background behind this shift, see Larry Siedentop: *Inventing the Individual: The Origins of Western Liberalism* (Cambridge, MA: The Belknap Press of Harvard University Press, 2014).
81. For Hobbes, this is the loss of life (see *Leviathan*, chapters 13-14); for Locke, this is the loss of property (see *Second Treatise of Government*, sec. 57 and 124). For a review of the scholarly literature on this change, see Riccardo Saccenti, *Debating Medieval Natural Law: A Survey* (Notre Dame, IN: University of Notre Dame Press, 2016).
82. This is the opinion of Joseph Ratzinger, "Truth and Freedom" *Communio* 23 (1996), 20: For Luther, the "issue was the freedom of conscience vis-à-vis the authority of the Church.... Even if it would not be right to speak of the individualism of the Reformation, the new importance of the individual and the shift in the relation between individual conscience and authority are nonetheless among its dominant traits."
83. Charles Morerod, OP, has argued that Protestant antirationalism is actually the foundation for political social contract theories characteristic of modernity because there is a direct connection between Luther's voluntarist idea of divine causality and the Hobbesian view in which every man is for himself alone, creating a war of all against all: "For Luther, 'God can only be everything, if man is nothing.' But man does not feel like nothing, and later would think it necessary to affirm himself against God." But to affirm oneself against God also implies affirming one's prerogative against one's neighbor. See *Ecumenism and Philosophy: Philosophical Questions for a Renewal of*

Dialogue, tr. by Therese C. Scarpelli (Ave Maria, FL: Sapientia Press, 2006), 103-115; quotation at 114.
84. Yet, we should also acknowledge that this never exculpates those who are so ignorant, for two reasons. First, the widespread and well-documented unhappiness of modernity should be prima facie evidence that our desires are not fulfilled when we focus on the self. Second, the more theoretical reflection of the intellect on the powers of human nature is still obligatory for anyone claiming to live the examined life. Nevertheless, if our society systematically embodies inordinate desires, then people are less often pulled out of themselves to make the examination.
85. Matthew Levering, *Biblical Natural Law: A Theocentric and Teleological Approach* (Oxford: Oxford University Press, 2008), 109; this comment was made of Rousseau, but applies equally to the other thinkers Levering analyzes: Hobbes, Locke, Hume, Rousseau, Kant, Hegel, and Nietzsche.
86. For example, where the replacement rate is 2.1 children per couple, the average fertility rate for the European Union as a whole in 2014 was 1.58, well below population-replacement level.
87. Augusto Del Noce, *The Crisis of Modernity*, tr. by Carlo Lancellotti (Montreal and Kingston: McGill-Queen's University Press, 2014).
88. Del Noce, "Violence and Modern Gnosticism" in *Crisis*, 24. He later (in "Authority versus Power," at 202) traces the source of this to Luther's *Bondage of the Will*, in which God's law is opposed to man's desire for happiness.
89. Del Noce, "Authority versus Power" in *Crisis*, 203: "Revolutionary atheism is the endpoint of a process that begins when in God the idea of power replaces the idea of authority.... Today's reality shows us that the eclipse of authority does not coincide at all with the advent of liberation, but rather with that of *power*, and totalitarian systems are the tangible expression of this substitution."
90. Del Noce, "Toward a New Totalitarianism" in *Crisis*, 87-91.
91. Del Noce, "Authority versus Power" in *Crisis*, 160.
92. Del Noce, "Authority versus Power" in *Crisis*, 233.
93. In short, the anti-Platonism that leads to a rejection of transcendence brings us directly back to Plato's portrayal of the tyrant as the least happy man because he is controlled by his appetites (*Republic* IX, 571a-579c).
94. As Archbishop Charles Chaput recently pointed out, "The crime of the modern sexual regime is that it robs Eros of its meaning and love of its grandeur" (Charles J. Chaput, *Strangers in a Strange Land: Living the Catholic Faith in a Post-Christian World* (New York: Henry Holt and Company, 2017), 101.
95. Robert Spaemann, *Basic Moral Concepts*, tr. by T.J. Armstrong (London: Routledge, 1989), 30-32.
96. Steven B. Smith, *Modernity and Its Discontents: Making and Unmaking the Bourgeois from Machiavelli to Bellow* (New Haven: Yale University Press, 2016), 13.

97. 1 Cor. 13:1-8.
98. Chaput, *Strangers*, 46.

Do Friends Need Justice or Do the Just Need Friendship? Natural Law as the Foundation for Justice and Friendship

Scott Jude Roniger

> But you, Perses, lay up these things within your heart and listen now to justice, ceasing altogether to think of violence. For the son of Cronos has ordained this law for men, that fishes and beasts and winged fowls should devour one another, for justice is not in them; but to mankind he gave justice which proves far the best.
>
> —Hesiod, *Works and Days*

"When men are friends they have no need of justice, while when they are just they need friendship as well, and the truest form of justice is found in friendship."[1] In this passage, Aristotle succinctly presents a nuanced picture of the manner in which justice and friendship structure the *polis* and the human agent's pursuit of *eudaimonia* within political life. In the space of a few lines, Aristotle lays out two important ideas with far-reaching implications. First, Aristotle says that friendship is "greater" than justice, so neither the polis nor the life of citizens is complete when only justice is present.[2] In order to cultivate and enjoy the complete or happy human life, the city and its inhabitants need to transcend the level of justice by developing friendships. Friends do not simply give what is owed to each other; rather, they try to "outdo" one another in giving benefits.[3] Therefore, those who stand to each other in a relationship of justice need friends, but friends do not need justice. Second, Aristotle claims that justice in its fullest sense is found in friendship.[4] We might gloss this last point by saying that justice is perfected, it reaches its *telos* or completion, in friendship, which is itself the perfection of political life.

These points gleaned from Aristotle's terse remarks raise important questions about the relationship between justice and friendship. Is justice a foundation for friendship? If so, how? If friends no longer have need of justice, then how are we to understand the claim that justice is perfected in friendship? Is justice perfected by being "removed" or "overcome" by friendship? In this essay, we will investigate the relationship between justice and friendship as articulated by Aristotle and developed by Thomas Aquinas, and we will pay special attention to the genesis of justice and friendship. That is, we will attempt to describe the foundations for the virtue of justice and the life of friendship. First, we will evaluate a recent attempt to articulate Aquinas's understanding of justice and friendship. Second, we will describe the ontological aspects of friendship and discuss how the being of friends bears upon the manner in which friends operate in their relationship, and we will show that Aristotle's understanding of a friend as a second self provides a basis for the claim that friendship transcends justice. Third, we will investigate the genesis of justice and friendship, paying special attention (a) to the role of natural law and temperance in the instantiation of justice and (b) to the fact that justice provides the soil in which friendship can take root.

A Recent Discussion of the Relationship between Justice and Friendship

Daniel Schwartz has written recently about the relationship between justice and friendship in the thought of Aquinas. His work represents a valuable contribution to the theme, but we will highlight aspects of his treatment that need to be adjusted.[5] We do not wish simply to discuss his work in order to disagree with his claims, although we will in fact disagree with his positions, but rather to use his discussion both to manifest important issues concerning the relationship between justice and friendship and to clarify our own position. We will focus our critique on two specific points.

Does Justice Remain within Friendship?

First, Schwartz claims that Aquinas's conception of friendship "coexists with conflict, disputes, and mutual uncertainties between friends."[6] He says that these disputes and conflicts are inalienable features of human relationships, and therefore "whatever the closeness present in a relationship, justice never becomes redundant."[7] Schwartz says that, for Aquinas, a common goal is both a requisite and effect of friendship, but even "the existence of a common goal does not assure an end to disputes."[8] He says that friendship requires a union of wills, but this union need only be formal, not formal and material. That is, the same goal must be willed by two friends precisely as a common goal (formally), but the friends can disagree about the ways to achieve this goal. They can will different ways to instantiate the goal and thus will different things "materially."[9] Such "material" disagreements are consistent with friendship, according to Schwartz. However, these disputes show that even friends need recourse to the demands of justice. The inevitable disagreements that occur in common action for common ends force even friends to stoop to the level of justice, or, even better, these disagreements lift the demands of justice into the essence of friendship. Thus, Schwartz concludes that justice is a constitutive part of friendship and "never becomes redundant."

Prima facie, this claim seems to be in tension with Aristotle's understanding of the relationship between friendship and justice. It is precisely Aristotle's point that friends no longer need recourse to the demands of justice; friends have transcended the level of being bound to what is simply owed to the other, even if justice is co-extensive with friendship.[10] However, we have already asked how we should understand the relation between Aristotle's claims that (1) friendship is superior to justice, such that friends no longer need justice, and (2) his somewhat enigmatic remark that justice in its fullest sense is an aspect of friendship. Schwartz's point that "material" disagreements amongst friends ensure the enduring necessity of justice seems to be a way to alleviate this tension. Friends have moved beyond justice until they disagree about the means to achieve common ends, at which point they revert to the demands of justice. Yet Aristotle seems to suggest a much different relationship between justice and friendship than that proposed by Schwartz. If the strictest form of justice is found within friendship, then it seems that justice is being given short shrift by Schwartz. Is the height of justice merely the respect that friends need to maintain for each other when confronted with "material" disagreements? My point is not simply to diagnose Schwartz's presentation of Thomas as possibly disagreeing with Aristotle on this issue, although that may be implied by his formulation. The more important point is the structure of justice and friendship according to Schwartz (or more specifically, according to Schwartz's Aquinas). In his view, friends never fully transcend the order of justice; justice endures within friendship as a kind of moral safety net.

What is the Genesis of Justice?

We now turn to the second relevant aspect of Schwartz's presentation of the relationship between justice and friendship, which concerns the genesis of the obligations of justice. We can put our question as follows: According to Schwartz, how do claims of justice, especially between agents who are unequal, originate? Basing himself on Aquinas's discussions of theological charity and merit, he concludes, "there is a sense in which friendship is not opposed to, but rather is a necessary feature of the circumstances in which it makes sense to invoke justice."[11] Further, he says that in situations where there is no strict equality between agents, the subordinate agent in the relationship has no way to generate a claim of justice until the superior agent produces a proportional equality between them through establishing a friendship. He says, "For your actions to generate a just claim on the giver you must be the recipient of the giver's love, which you are if you are a friend of the giver."[12] Again, he argues, "Friendship introduces proportional equivalence among the actions of unequals by making the actions of the partners common to both friends."[13] On this account, without the superior agent's gracious extension of friendship to the inferior agent, the inferior simply has no claim of justice in the relationship.

With the intention of illustrating Aquinas's thought, Schwartz applies these principles philosophically to an imagined political situation. He asks us to imagine two countries, one extremely powerful and affluent, Opulenta, and one extremely poor and weak, Terrapovera. Due to the vast disparity between the relative wealth and power of these nations, Schwartz says, "The inequality between the countries is so extreme that *no just exchange can take place*. In fact, the value of the actions of Terrapovera and Opulenta belongs to different orders altogether."[14] Schwartz then asks us to imagine that Terrapovera freely decides to join one of Opulenta's projects, and Opulenta decides to share some of its resources with the struggling nation. According to Schwartz, it is only Opulenta's actions in sharing its assets that lifts Terrapovera to a level where justice can be obtained between the two countries. Only because of Opulenta's generosity is Terrapovera entitled to any claims of justice in its relations with Opulenta. He says, "Now [after Opulenta's unnecessary sharing with Terrapovera] both countries can engage in exchange of a kind such that we can call just or unjust; they are now also in a situation in which they can engage in cooperation and friendship."[15] One is relieved that Opulenta is so gracious; given Schwartz's claim that "no just exchange can take place" between the countries before Opulenta's supererogatory offer of assistance, one could just as easily imagine the powerful nation saying to Terrapovera, "The strong do what they can and the weak suffer what they must."[16] In any case, Schwartz concludes, "Friendship establishes relations of justice between unequal partners by introducing proportional equivalence in their actions, and thus introducing some kind of equality."[17] On his view of Aquinas, becoming a subject of justice is concomitant with becoming a friend, at least in a situation where the two parties are not originally in a relationship of strict equality.

Finally, Schwartz stipulates that his reading of Aquinas "does not lend support to the notion that friendship takes precedence over justice ('you only have justice if you have friendship first')."[18] His reasoning for this claim is that in the "transition from a superior-inferior relationship to a relationship between partners, friendship and the possibility of just interaction arise concomitantly."[19] Despite his claims to the contrary, we are left to wonder how friendship does not take precedence over justice. In the example of the two disparate nations, Schwartz's point was precisely that there was no justice possible between the countries until Opulenta offered the olive branch of friendship. At the very least, there seems to be a conceptual and ontological, if not temporal, priority of friendship over justice. In the following two sections, we will respond to both of Schwartz's points by drawing from Aristotle, Aquinas, and the work of Robert Sokolowski.

Friendship as the Perfection of Justice

In this section, we will respond to Schwartz's claim that justice is always necessary within friendship. We begin by recalling his position that "Whatever the closeness of the relationship (i.e. friendship), justice never becomes redundant." Is it true that justice remains even within friendship? Should we interpret Aristotle's dictum that justice in its truest sense is found within friendship to mean that *justice itself* remains between friends? Our response to these questions will unfold in two subsections. In the first subsection, we will explore the ontology of friendship by appealing to Aquinas's understanding of the relation between being and operation and Aristotle's idea that a friend is a second self. In the second subsection, we will discuss how this ontology of friendship expresses itself in moral actions between friends. This second point can be seen as a phenomenological enhancement of what it means *to be* friends. If we are friends, how do situations that call for common action show up to us? Is this manifestation within friendship different from the way situations that call for justice manifest themselves?

The Ontology of Friendship

A fundamental theme in Aquinas's philosophy is that an entity acts according to the mode of being that it possesses. That is, action always follows upon being; what an entity is sets the trajectory for its characteristic operations. Aquinas says, "Since nothing operates except insofar as it is actualized (*est actu*), each entity's mode of operating (*modus operandi*) follows upon its mode of being (*modus essendi ipsius*)."[20] As an entity is, so it acts. To illuminate this point, one might also appeal to Thomas's metaphysics of formal causality. Substantial forms give *esse* and are a source of inclinations to the proper activities and ends of the entity, and accidental forms give *esse* and inclinations that can facilitate the agent's achievements of its proper ends.[21] For Aquinas, therefore, the principle that the mode of operation follows upon the mode of being holds not only for the substantial being of an entity. It is not only that the "doggy" mode of operation follows upon the "doggy" mode of being and the human mode of operation from the human mode of being. This principle also holds at the level of virtue and character. To be virtuous is to have developed a way of being that enables one to perceive what is fitting for a human agent and that inclines one to choose freely those actions conducive to the perfection of human nature.

To elucidate this point, it is helpful to turn to Aristotle's discussion of virtuous moral action and skillful performances. Concerning the development of skills, Aristotle says, "It is possible to do something grammatical either by chance of under the guidance of another. A man will be proficient in grammar, then, only when he has both done something grammatical and done it grammatically; and this means doing it in accordance with the grammatical knowledge within himself."[22] To alter Aristotle's example, the skillful doctor not only makes the correct medical decision, but he also does it "medically"; he acts *as* a skillful doctor acts. The existence of the "medical" act is not enough to show that the agent has the proper skill; he must also do it from the skill, the stable ability to perform excellently, he has developed.

The same structure manifest in the acquisition of skills also holds in the development of virtues. Aristotle says that an action may be morally upright, but this fact alone does not guarantee that the agent himself is just or temperate. A right action does not necessarily entail a virtuous character. For the action to be virtuous, the agent must "be in a certain condition when he acts." He must act with knowledge, choose the act for its own sake, and the act "must proceed from a firm and unchangeable character."[23] Aristotle says, "Actions then are called just and temperate when they are such as the just or the temperate man would do; but it is not the man who does these that is just and temperate, but the man who also does them as just and temperate men do them."[24] Thus, the courageous man's actions must not only align with the demands of the noble in the face of danger, but they must also proceed from the *hexis*, or as Yves Simon says, the "existential readiness" to perform those actions courageously.[25] By facing many fearful situations that call for firm and principled responses, a person develops the "existential readiness" of courage. At the outset of his moral development, he performed the right action, but he did not perform it courageously. Upon achieving the "existential readiness" of courage, he is now able to confidently and creatively respond to hardships. In doing so, his actions are no longer simply correct; they are now courageous. He does the courageous action courageously.

    The key is to understand a *hexis, habitus,* or existential readiness as "midway" between mere potency and full actuality.[26] A *habitus* is an actualization of an ability to develop the *habitus* in question, but the same *habitus* also functions as a potency in relation to the fully energized activities that flow from the *habitus*. Vernon Bourke says that a *habitus* for Aquinas is "not a mere automatic conditioning of a power as the modern term 'habit' connotes but the metaphysical growth of a basic potency for operation."[27] The proper understanding of a *habitus* reveals the dynamic character of a virtue; it is geared toward a certain kind of action, like a coiled spring. Therefore, in the courageous actions of a virtuous agent, we see Aquinas's principle (the mode of operation follows upon the mode of being) manifest in the moral life. The metaphysical growth from a potency to a *habitus* or existential readiness alters the mode of being of the agent. We might say that the courageous person's life has been expanded by the development of the virtue, and, as such, his mode of operation also changes. He does not simply do the brave thing; he also performs it courageously.

Aristotle employs these examples to illustrate the development of skills and virtues. He moves "from the bottom up" by clarifying how the same material actions done by a novice and by a master are actually quite different in their quality, since the actions of the master are not generating the skill but flowing from it. The distinction that enables us to see the same action as qualitatively different because it flows from a different source also enables us to unravel the knot concerning the relationship between justice and friendship. Schwartz says that justice remains necessary because friends inevitably disagree or run into rough patches in their relationship, and such tribulations are compatible with friendship because justice remains between them. On his account, friends have recourse to the demands of justice, such as respecting the differing opinion of an interlocutor. However, Schwartz misses the crucial point that operation follows upon being.

The relationship between friends is such that their being has been altered in relationship to each other; friendship is a kind of virtue or existential readiness, or at least it accompanies such virtue. Again, we might say that the lives of friends have been changed or *enlarged*. As long as their friendship lasts, they are no longer simply two persons in relation to each other. Rather, a friend is "another self" because of the virtues the friends have developed in their pursuit of common goods.[28] Most fundamentally, to call a friend "another self" is not to see one's own virtues replicated or objectified in one's friend; a friend is not another self primarily because I see myself in him or because he enables me to see myself for what I really am. Rather, Aryeh Kosman says, "The fact that my friend enjoys a kinship of similarity with me is true and of interest insofar as *he enables the enlargement of my being*, not insofar as he replicates and objectifies it. Since my friend is like me but separate, *we are able to constitute a community of shared activity* that goes beyond and amplifies the experience of each of us separately. It is solidarity and not reflexivity with which sodality is linked."[29] A friend is "another I," not just another me, with whom I form a community (*koinonia*), or a "we-subject," based on the shared vision and pursuit of common goods. The most important of these common goods, including the friendship itself, the pursuits of which are constitutive of friendship, are goods that are not diminished but intensified in the sharing of them.

However, it is not only that my subjective being is enhanced or enlarged in friendship. Through my friend, precisely because we co-perceive reality, think, speak, and act together, "I acquire a wider, deeper, and more powerful range of *objective* conscious life."[30] Kosman says that through friendship "the enhancement of my being not simply as subject but as objectively determined consciousness is accomplished by the richer field of objective being made possible by political life, that is, by the life of friendship."[31] Friends enlarge their being by enabling each other to encounter intelligently a wider field of reality. They open up new vistas for each other.

Since, according to Aquinas, the mode of operation follows upon the mode of being, the enhanced being that I enjoy through friendships also transforms the mode in which I operate toward my friend. Schwartz may be correct that friends will periodically disagree; one may even need to be admonished by a friend, as Cicero reminds us.[32] Schwartz is also correct that the friendship survives these disagreements and admonitions. However, such disagreements are not compatible with friendship because the disagreeing friends revert to the level of justice, which survives within friendship. Rather, these respectful disagreements and admonitions are themselves acts of friendship, and precisely for this reason they are at the same time the fulfillment or perfection of justice. Friends have indeed transcended the realm of justice; they are not bound to each other solely in the mode of giving to each what is owed, and they do not have to invoke the rules of justice to regulate their interactions. On the one hand, transactions of justice demand that the people interacting be related simply as two persons, not as "second selves." On the other hand, the actions of friends are qualitatively different from those who act out of respect for justice. The actions of friends flow from a different source; they are expressions of the reciprocated love and shared vision of a community of those who mutually will the good of the other for the other's sake in the pursuit of common goods, and therefore they do not stem from individuals or groups in need of the calibrations of justice. Lady Justice is blind, but the love of friends is not.

The same material action can therefore be an act of justice in one setting but an act of friendship in another. Two strangers from different countries may find themselves in a situation that calls for mutual respect in the face of differing opinions about a pressing question, and in this case the granting of such respect would indeed be an act of justice. However, the same act of respecting the different opinion of an interlocutor is primarily an act of friendship when it occurs between two virtuous friends at a town hall meeting. Because the friends have altered and enhanced their being, they act not out of "respect" for each other and for the law that regulates their interactions but rather from a love for each other that has matured over time.[33] It is precisely because they have transcended the laws of justice that their actions are the perfection of justice, since both justice and friendship aim at harmony or concord. Contra Schwartz, friends do not need recourse to justice, but friendship elevates and perfects the demands of justice.[34] Friendship achieves in an eminent way what justice implements at the genesis of social life.

The Moral Identifications within Friendship

The enlarged being of friends and hence their enhanced mode of operating toward each other enables them to act in ways that transcend but do not violate the demands of justice. This point can be clarified by discussing the kind of thinking that animates moral actions. To this end, Robert Sokolowski's insight into the human ability "to take an object or action as" will be helpful.[35] Sokolowski distinguishes between human moral actions and mere "material performances." An example will enable us to illustrate this distinction. We can imagine a young girl running into a street to retrieve a ball that was kicked from her front yard. While the girl is pursuing the ball, a car speeds down the street, and its driver does not see the girl. If I deliberately and aggressively push the young girl in order to remove her from the path of the speeding car, I have done a morally good action, and I deserve praise. However, if I deliberately and aggressively push the same girl because she is disturbing me with her childish nattering while I am trying to sleep on a plane, I have done a morally despicable action, and I deserve blame and legal punishment. In both cases, the material performance, the pushing, is the same, but the moral qualities of the respective actions are quite different.

Sokolowski identifies "what is added" to a material performance to make it a moral action. He says, "The material performance, while it is going on and in addition to going on, is also recognized or identified (1) as being my, the agent's performance, and (2) as being good or bad to those toward whom it is done. What is added to the performance is a form of recognition, a 'being identified as' or 'being recognized as.'"[36] According to Sokolowski, "A moral transaction . . . is a human performance that is informed by moral categoriality, the form of identification in which I take and do the good or bad of another, as such, as my own good or bad."[37] If I identify my performance of pushing the young girl as good for her because it saves her life, and, taking it as good for her, I do it as my good, as that which obliges me as a human being, then I am acting bravely towards her. If, however, I identify the pushing as bad for her and do it as my good (due to my anger at her incessant nattering), then I have assaulted her. The array of forms of moral behavior opens up once a human agent begins to identify someone's good or bad, as such, as his good or bad.

We can build on Sokolowski's theme of moral identification by applying it to justice and friendship. Aquinas defines justice as "the habit whereby one gives to each what is his due by a constant and perpetual will."[38] In situations that call for justice there must be three factors present: (1) a giver, the person who is obligated, (2) a recipient to whom something belongs, and (3) the thing given and received, which can be an object, a liberty, a responsibility, an immunity, etc. Thus, justice is a tripartite relationship that culminates in an action whereby one renders what is due to another. In this triangulation, the moral agent, the giver, always identifies the two parties (himself and the receiver) "as a two" that need to have their relationship equilibrated by the giving and receiving of what is owed. The thing given and received *is taken as owed to the recipient*, and it is identified and given *as his*.[39] The thing given is good for the recipient insofar as it is owed to him, and the act of giving is good for the giver insofar as it calibrates the relationship. In justice, the primary mode of identification is that of obligation. If John owes Kevin $5, because of the way that John, the giver, and Kevin, the recipient, are related to each other and to the reality that must be exchanged, then John must take that reality as belonging to Kevin, as owed to him. In justice, the situation that presents itself to the just agent is already textured by the relationships involved, and therefore it demands a certain action.

When one moves to the realm of friendship, the identification, or the "taking as," changes. Because friends are related as second selves, the goods "exchanged" in friendship are not identified as owed to another as his, even if they may in fact be owed. Rather, the goods that are exchanged are wanted for the friend for the friend's sake, and precisely as such the agent sees the moral transaction as his own good. That is, the friend's good for the friend's sake is seen as the good of the agent; he takes himself and his friend as a kind of "one," or as a hendiadys, a one through two. As Aristotle says, rectified self-love is the source of the love of friendship because virtuous agents want that which is perfective of their friends just as they want those things for themselves.[40]

In friendship, therefore, I take that which is good for my friend for his sake as *good for us*. The enlarged and enhanced being of friends enables them to identify goods in this new and elevated way. I identify some good not as owed to you, but first and foremost as perfective of you and hence good for us, since we are now an intimate communion of persons. The moral vision of friends is not limited to the narrower focus of what is owed to the other. Rather, friends actively search for what is good for each other, and therefore they are free to pursue a wider range of goods together. Thus, friends do not merely respond to situations that present themselves but are more creative in their pursuit of common goods. If justice is a relationship that culminates in an act, then friendship is a mode of life punctuated by actions that enable a community to pursue creatively common goods that grow as they are shared. Therefore, even if the same material performance occurs as an act of justice in one setting and an act of friendship in another, the moral categoriality involved will be different. In Schwartz's example of friends in a disagreement, it is not that they maintain just dealings with each other through their differences by identifying respect as owed to the other. Rather, they identify the argument conducted civilly as good for them as they pursue the truth about the good.

Natural Law and Justice as the Soil for Friendship

We can now respond to the second point we highlighted in Schwartz's work: his claim that it is only friendship between unequal agents that brings about the possibility of justice between them. As we discussed above, he says that Terrapovera can only be a subject of justice in its relations with Opulenta if Opulenta first establishes friendship between the two countries. I suggest that the order of justice and friendship is exactly the reverse, and in this section I will give my account of the way in which justice provides a foundation for friendship. It is justice which enables the establishment of harmony in the form of proportional equality between unequals, that establishes the possibility of friendship, and justice itself is based upon the natural law. Justice, built upon the natural law, is the "soil" in which friendship can take root.

We can distinguish two ways in which justice provides a foundation for friendship: it instantiates (1) harmony in the soul of the agent and (2) harmony between the agent and other human beings. Aristotle's qualified identification of virtue with justice "as a whole," or general justice, can help us see the two ways in which justice undergirds friendship. Aristotle says, "Virtue is the same as [general] justice, but what it is to be virtue is not the same as what it is to be justice. Rather, insofar as virtue is related to another, it is justice, and insofar as it is a certain sort of state (*hexis*) without qualification, it is virtue."[41] Justice can therefore be spoken of in two ways. Insofar as justice is an actualization of the human agent's capacities such that it gives one the existential readiness to do justice and to desire what is just, it is a virtue that perfects the agent himself and rectifies his appetites. Insofar as justice is the ability to identify and establish the proper kind of equality between people and groups by giving to each his due, then justice, considered as justice, perfects the relationships between people and "seems to be another person's good, because it is related to another; for it does what benefits another."[42] Because justice perfects the agent by calibrating and rectifying his social and political interactions, it straddles the distinction between immanent and transitive activity so crucial to Aristotle's *Metaphysics*.[43] Considered as a virtue, it is an immanent activity that remains "within" and perfects the agent; considered as justice it is a transitive activity that "stretches out to" and perfects the social and political fabric of one's life.

Justice is a foundation for friendship in both of these senses because it perfects the agent by enabling him to harmonize the social and political interactions necessary for human development and happiness. As virtue, it perfects the soul of the agent and roots out, or wards off, any pleonexic tendencies that would vitiate the possibility of complete friendship. As justice, it harmonizes the relationships between people and provides the backdrop from which friendship can make its appearance. Further, justice, considered as itself and as a virtue, is rooted in the natural law. As Aristotle says, general justice must be understood in relation to the (positive) law, but the law itself must be rooted in that which is good by nature. In the following subsections, we will discuss the manner in which the natural law provides the foundation for (a) justice as a virtue and (b) justice as the proper relations between agents. We will sketch a hierarchy in which natural law is ordered toward justice, which is then foundational for friendship.[44]

Natural Law and Virtue

The ancient and medieval tradition largely held that law is enacted in order to inculcate virtue among the citizens of a given community. Both positive law and natural law were understood as foundations for virtue or even training in virtue, and virtues in turn bring out the full dynamism and intelligibility of law. We can recapitulate this understanding of the connection between natural law and virtue by appealing to Sokolowski's and Francis Slade's definition of natural law. Sokolowski and Slade argue that the natural law can be defined as *"the ontological priority of ends over purposes."*[45] I wish to suggest that this definition shows what is first in the order of discovery, as distinct from what is first in the order of being; it is first "for us" and as such has an especially important role in our discussion of the natural law as a foundation for justice and friendship. In order to discover the natural law as the ontological priority of ends over purposes, we must learn to distinguish between three things: (1) the ends of entities we use and encounter (including the ends of human nature), (2) our purposes in making our decisions, and (3) the positive laws and customs of our community. Once we make these distinctions, we can see that we are measured, not by our own purposes, but first and foremost by the ends of things, especially the ends of human nature. The distinctions between ends, purposes, and customs therefore enable one to align one's actions with that which is fitting for the ends of human nature, thereby facilitating the development of virtue.

To show how the natural law, understood as the ontological priority of ends over purposes and customs, directs human agents toward virtue, we must specify what we mean by "end" as a recapitulation of Aristotle's conception of *telos*. The end of an entity is its characteristic, native excellence. Ends are "in" things; ends "come about concomitantly with the things they belong to. Things might spring into being when they are generated or made or occur by accident, but ends do not arise without the thing. An end is the finished, perfected state of a thing, the thing when it is acting well as what it is."[46] Aristotle expresses the connection between the nature of an entity and its *telos* or perfection when discussing a polity. He says, "Every city, therefore, exists by nature, if such also are the first communities. For the city is their end, and nature is an end: what each thing is — for example, a human being, a horse, or a household — when its coming into being is complete is, we assert, the nature of that thing. Again, that for the sake of which a thing exists, or the end, is what is best; and self-sufficiency is an end and what is best."[47] The nature or end of a thing is that thing enjoying its completion; the nature of a thing is its *telos*. The *telos* of a thing is the *eidos* as most fully actualized and thus as most fully itself.

Natural ends exist independently of human purposes; ends are "in" things, but human purposes come into being only when human agents formulate intentions for their actions. While ends are "in" things independently of our decisions concerning them, our purposes or intentions are up to us, as Aristotle says. Aristotle argues that we can wish for impossible things, we can wish for things that are possible but not by our own agency, and we can wish for things that we can bring about by ourselves or with our friends.[48] When this last form of wishing begins to direct our moral deliberations and conduct, such wishes become purposes. Sokolowski says, "*Purposes* or *intentions* are wishes that have kicked into action."[49] Purposes are what we set down for ourselves; purposes are our intentions in acting, and as such they only come about with our thinking and willing. "Purposes, therefore, can exist only in human beings. . . . There are purposes only in the strict sense when there are men."[50] We are the rulers of our purposes and thus free to devise them as we direct our actions, but we cannot change the ends of things. I may intend to use language to lie or manipulate others so as to attain my desires, but I simply cannot make the end, or perfection, of speech itself to be deception.[51] Therefore, our freedom in setting our purposes carries a natural responsibility to align our intentions with the ends of things. By recognizing and responding to the priority of ends over purposes, human agents are set on the path to virtue.

For the natural law to function as a foundation for virtue, a similar distinction must be made between the ends of things and the positive laws or customs of our community (between *physis* and *nomos*). The ends of entities come into sharper focus for us when we are able to see them as distinct from both our purposes and also the customs of our culture. The laws of a country may respect the ends of things or they may vitiate them, but the discovery of the natural law entails seeing that the natural goodness of things is more fundamental than the laws of a community. This distinction often arises when the positive laws are opposed to some natural end or when these laws are inadequate in some domain of human action, but the distinction need not manifest itself in a state of conflict between the natural end and the established law of the land. The key is to distinguish what is good by nature, what fits with the ends of the thing in question, and what is good by legal decree or culture. It requires seeing what Aristotle calls the naturally just as the foundation for the legally just.[52] It is simply good to tell the truth to a jury in a legal proceeding, and the goodness of this action is confirmed but not originally established by positive laws forbidding perjury. Also, the goodness of honest speaking is distinct in kind from the goodness of paying one's taxes at the appointed deadline, although both are in fact good. Distinguishing these dimensions of goodness is an achievement of human intelligence through which reason, directed by natural law, sheds light on the path to virtue.

While the natural law directs human agents toward the development of a virtuous character, it is the morally virtuous agent, the *studioso* in Aquinas's Latin, who manifests the truth of things and allows the truth about the good to be normative for his actions. He is the one who most vividly shows how the natural law is ordered to the inculcation of virtue. Aquinas describes law as a rule and measure for human actions. Additionally, both Aristotle and Aquinas describe the virtuous person (*spoudaios* or *studioso*) as a "rule and measure" for human actions.[53] The virtuous person is a rule and measure for action because he embodies and perfects the natural law, and thus his actions manifest both the law itself and the perfection of the law, namely virtue.[54] Both Aristotle and Aquinas recognize that, although things are what they are independently of our thinking about them, everyone sees the world through the prism of his own character. It is the good, virtuous agent who can see the world as it really is; he is the measure of the truth of things because he submits himself to the way things show themselves.[55]

Kevin Flannery says that the truth associated with the virtuous and practically wise person is "practical truth or truth bound up with getting *to* things."[56] We can add that the practically wise person gets "to the truth of things" by identifying and respecting the ends or perfections of things. He responds quickly, intelligently, and creatively to the ends of things while allowing those ends to form his purposes in acting, and his performances show what the natural law is by revealing that it is meant to shape a virtuous human character. Thus, the virtuous agent witnesses to the ends of things by shaping his purposes to be in line with or to bring about the native excellences of entities. Above all, the practically wise person loves and actualizes the ends of human nature in the exercise of virtue. He moves from discovering and responding to a natural rule and measure for human action to being a rule and measure for human action. In this way, the natural law as the ontological priority of ends over purposes and customs serves as a foundation for virtue.

By recognizing and respecting the natural law as the ontological priority of ends over purposes, human agents are free to develop virtues, and I wish to suggest that the virtue of temperance plays a crucial role in the development and maintenance of justice. Aristotle presents lust and gluttony as the two great enemies of justice.[57] If left undisciplined, the desires for food, drink, and sex, which can be regulated and made to share more fully in human intelligence by the virtue of temperance, become opposed to justice because: (1) gluttony inclines one to take more than one needs, and (2) lust inclines one to what belongs directly to someone else (the body of another). In both gluttony and lust, we are led to prefer more for ourselves at the expense of what is owed to another, and these unruly appetites eventually lead to unjust actions. As Aristotle says, human beings often commit unjust actions "for the enjoyment and the satisfaction of desire. For if they have a desire beyond the necessary things, they will commit injustice in order to cure it – and not only for this reason, for they might desire merely the enjoyment that comes with pleasures unaccompanied by pains."[58] Temperance not only undergirds and preserves prudence, as Aristotle explicitly says, but it also undergirds and preserves justice.[59]

Whereas lust, gluttony, and injustice lead a person to take for himself what belongs to another, justice works for the "good of the other" by giving what is owed to the other.[60] The achievement of temperance, founded on the recognition that the ends of human nature and social life have priority over one's desires, liberates one from the forms of behavior that lead to injustice. Temperance establishes an order in the appetites of the person that makes him capable of the virtue of justice. Justice is therefore a "social virtue" that depends upon the rectified appetites of its members.

Contra Schwartz, it is not friendship that initially enables the claims of justice to be identified and respected, but temperance rooted in the natural law. Returning to his example, we can now say that Opulenta's recognition of the natural law (the priority of ends over purposes and customs) and its temperate pursuit of goods would ensure that it did not take advantage of Terrapovera. As temperance takes root in the soul of a person (or nation), his mind is freed to correctly perceive how goods, services, honors, and responsibilities should be justly arranged. Further, Schwartz seems to suggest that friendship not only enables justice to take place but also "creates" the claims of justice. On our interpretation, temperance does not "create" the claims of justice, which are in place by the nature and ends of the things involved, but temperance does free human agents from inordinate desires that would occlude their vision of what justice requires or hinder their pursuit of it. Temperance enables us to identify and respond to the situations that call for justice; it clears the fog of unruly desire, but justice is demanded by the nature of the situation that confronts us. These virtues, rooted in the natural law, perfect the human agent and make him capable of friendship.

Natural Law and Justice as Harmony between Agents

Justice considered as a virtue is an immanent activity founded on the natural law and perfective of the human agent himself; it makes him worthy of complete friendship. Justice considered as justice is a transitive activity that establishes harmony between people and groups and therefore provides the social-political framework within which friendship can develop. We now turn to a brief discussion of this second dimension of justice and how it is founded on the natural law.

As we discussed in the first section, Schwartz claims that "the inequality between [Opulenta and Terrapovera] is so extreme that *no just exchange can take place*" prior to Opulenta's offer of friendship. However, the natural law as the ontological priority of ends over purposes and customs discloses the natural obligations that bind Opulenta even before friendship is established. Terrapovera, as an independent political community, has its own nature and ends that oblige Opulenta, or any other polity, in their interactions. The natural end of Terrapovera is the common good and happiness of its members, and this end has a natural priority over Opulenta's purposes, whatever they may be. The recognition of this end is the dawning of an obligation to align one's purposes with it, and the perception of the priority of this end is the mind's awakening to the attractive force of the noble (*to kalon*). A stronger nation's actions in relation to a weaker one are bounded by the ends of what it is to be a nation, not merely by the purpose of offering a gratuitous act of friendship; this natural tempering of action is the manifestation of the natural law and therefore the disclosure of the demands of justice. Given the kind of thing that Terrapovera is, a nation with the natural end of communal happiness, it would be a violation of natural law, and hence unjust, for Opulenta to interact with them in any way that would violate that end. Justice is demanded by the nature of things, by their being and ends, not by spontaneous offers of friendship, and therefore it is the natural law that enables a "just exchange can take place" between the two nations.

The recognition of the natural law enables individuals or nations to act in such a way as to create the harmony and equality characteristic of justice. By allowing ends to take priority over purposes, the relationships between people and groups are calibrated. The natural law prepares the ground for community life, and, by harmonizing the relationships between individuals and groups, justice provides the foundation for the edifice of friendship. By honoring the ends of Terrapovera, Opulenta would be acting justly towards the struggling nation and therefore creating the kind of relationship that could eventually develop into something like a friendship, although Aristotle says that friendships between cities generally remain at the level of utility.[61]

These points concerning the role of justice as a foundation for friendship can be further illuminated by Aristotle's remarks concerning the relationships amongst citizens and rulers within a polity. Aristotle understands the good *polis* to be a well-ordered community, and the role of the politician-legislator is to establish and maintain this order.[62] He links justice within the *polis* to (1) order (*taxis*), embedded within and flowing from (2) the constitution (*politeia*), and (3) law (*nomos*), which is determined by the form of the constitution.[63] He argues that friendship is possible amongst citizens to the extent that justice is present in their polity, and this sense of justice clearly includes the proper ordering (*taxis*) of the rulers to the ruled as well as an intelligent organization of the offices of the city in view of the common good.[64] He therefore shows that the kind of community obtaining amongst people tempers the demands of justice between them and hence the possibility of friendship amongst them.[65] Justice must be realized in any polity, but the demands of justice will be different in a monarchy, where justice is achieved in an eminent way, and in a timocracy (or polity), where justice is present but not as extensive or as intense as in the other good regimes. Aristotle is explicit that as justice increases so too does friendship.[66] Concerning the deviant regimes, Aristotle says that friendship is not possible in a tyranny precisely because there is no justice present in such a polity.[67] Thus, as political justice, founded upon that which is good by nature, harmonizes the relationships and interactions of citizens, friendships are able to develop and flourish; conversely, friendships are possible to the extent that justice harmonizes the common life of human beings. Therefore, justice understood as harmony between human agents is the soil within which friendship can take root.

Given the points we have made, we can say that justice is a kind of training for friendship. It harmonizes both the desires of the agent and the relationships between people; justice is the beginning, the baseline of community life that creates the conditions within which friendship can take root. We could go so far as to say that justice between citizens is equivalent to civic friendship, which would entail a distinction between civic friendship and virtuous or perfect friendship.[68] We can be just, and hence civic friends, to many individuals and groups, but we can only develop complete friendships with a few.[69] However, without the ability to recognize the priority of ends over purposes and customs and the existential readiness to give each his due, we could not reach the apex of moral life, which is the ability to identify our own good in loving another and willing the good for him for his sake. Thus, Aristotle presents a kind of ladder of happiness in the *Nicomachean Ethics*, in which justice is a preparation for the shared being, consciousness, and activity of friendship.

Finally, we should not think of these two aspects of justice, its being a virtue and its being a harmonious relationship between people and groups, as unrelated to each other. Aristotle argues repeatedly that the laws and the order of the city are meant to inculcate virtue in citizens.[70] As political animals, human beings must be brought up with proper laws that aid the development of virtues, and virtue in turn is understood in relation to and as a perfection of the law. Further, happiness requires that human beings participate virtuously in the various subsidiary spheres of social and political life. Thus, virtue enables the harmony needed for human happiness and a well-functioning polity, and the order of the polity, structured by intelligent law, inculcates virtue in the members of that community. Virtue and the harmonious order of community life mutually influence each other.

Conclusion

Schwartz's work attempts to tackle a subtle and important topic. His presentation of justice and friendship falls short in at least two ways, but his claims raise important questions and assist us in discussing essential topics in moral and political philosophy. In closing, we should add that, according to Aristotle, love and goodwill are both natural to human beings and at the origin of social and political life, along with need and expediency. Aristotle is not a proto-Hobbesian; he sees human beings as naturally friendly, and therefore natural law and justice are necessary not to restrain otherwise violent, anti-social beings but to elevate a natural love for other humans by harmonizing common actions for common ends, thereby facilitating human interactions in which people jointly pursue that which is fitting for human nature.[71] Further, according to St. Thomas, an end (*finis*) of law is friendship, either between human beings themselves or between human beings and God.[72] The natural law, which protects and promotes the achievements of the ends of human nature in familial, social, and political life based on the loving search for truth and happiness, reaches its fulfillment in virtuous friendships between human agents and between human beings and God. Law achieves its end of promoting friendship by inculcating the virtues, especially justice, in human agents, thus elevating the practical reasoning of human beings and making them capable of higher levels of communion. Law and justice prepare the way for friendship.[73]

Notes

1. Aristotle, *Nicomachean Ethics* (NE), VIII.1, 1155a25-28. I consult and modify the translation found in Aristotle, *Nicomachean Ethics*, trans. Terence Irwin (Cambridge: Hackett Publishing Company, 1999).
2. Aristotle discusses the need for "works of friendship" within a city at *Politics*, III.9. Translations of the *Politics* are from Aristotle, *Politics*, trans. Carnes Lord (Chicago: The University of Chicago Press, 2013).
3. See *NE*, VIII.13, 1162b5-15.
4. John Cooper translates the final clause in Aristotle's sentence as "The strictest form of justice is found in friendship." See John Cooper, "Political Animals and Civic Friendship," in *Friendship: A Philosophical Reader*, ed. Neera Badhwar (London: Cornell University Press, 1993), 321.

5. See Daniel Schwartz Porzecanski, "Friendship and the Circumstances of Justice According to Aquinas," Daniel Schwartz in *The Review of Politics* 66 (2004): 35-54. A version of the article also appears as Chapter 6 of *Aquinas on Friendship* (Oxford: Clarendon Press, 2007), 123-141.
6. Schwartz Porzecanski, "Friendship and the Circumstances of Justice According to Aquinas," *The Review of Politics* 66 (2004): 35.
7. *Ibid.*
8. *Ibid.*, 38.
9. *Ibid.*, 38-39. For a discussion of the distinction between formal and material union of wills and the way this distinction bears upon friendship, see Daniel Schwartz Porzecanski, "Aquinas on Concord: 'Concord Is a Union of Wills, Not of Opinions,'" *The Review of Metaphysics* 57 (2003): 25-42.
10. See *NE*, VII.9-11.
11. *Ibid.*, 47.
12. *Ibid.*, 50.
13. *Ibid.*, 51.
14. *Ibid.* Emphasis added.
15. *Ibid.*, 52. Parenthesis added.
16. Thucydides, *History of the Peloponnesian War*, 5.89.
17. Schwartz Porzecanski, "Friendship and the Circumstances of Justice," 53.
18. *Ibid.*, 54.
19. *Ibid.*
20. *Summa theologiae* (*St*), I, q. 89, a. 1.
21. For the principle that form gives being, see *Summa Contra Gentiles* (SCG), II, c. 55. Aquinas says, "Being (*esse*) accompanies form through itself." See also *St*, I, q. 75, a. 6. For the principle that form gives inclination, see *St*, I, q. 80, a. 1: "Some inclination follows upon every form." See also *St*, I-II, q. 94, a. 3.
22. *NE*, II.4, 1105a21-25.
23. *NE*, II.4, 1105a30-35.
24. *NE*, II.4, 1105b5-10.
25. Simon translates *hexis* and *habitus* as "existential readiness." See Yves Simon, *The Definition of Moral Virtue*, ed. Vukan Kuic (New York: Fordham University Press, 1986), 71-79.
26. See *St*, I-II, q. 71, a. 3: "Habitus medio modo se habet inter potentiam et actuum purum."
27. Vernon Bourke, "The Role of Habitus in the Thomistic Metaphysics of Potency and Act," in *Essays in Thomism*, ed. Robert E. Brennan (New York: Sheed and Ward, 1942), 106.
28. For the description of a friend as "another self," see Aristotle, *NE*, IX.4, 1166a30-32. Of course, in this section and the next we are discussing what Aristotle calls complete or perfect friendships, the friendships of the virtuous.

29. Aryeh Kosman, *Virtues of Thought: Essays on Plato and Aristotle* (Cambridge, MA: Harvard University Press, 2014), 174. Emphasis added. The title of the chapter in which this quote appears is "Aristotle on the Desirability of Friends."
30. *Ibid.*, 179.
31. *Ibid.*
32. See Cicero, *Laelius de Amicitia*, Ch. 24-26. However, Aristotle says that disagreements are characteristic of friendships based on pleasure or utility, not virtue. See *NE*, VIII.13. See *NE*, IX.12, 1172a10-15 for Aristotle's statement that in friendships of "decent" people the friends improve each other through mutual corrections.
33. See *St*, I-II, q. 26, a. 4 for Aquinas's distinction between *amor amicitiae* and *amor concupiscentiae*. See David Gallagher, "Thomas Aquinas on Self-Love as the Basis for Love of Others," *Acta Philosophica*, 8 (1999): 22-44.
34. See *NE*, VIII.9, 1159b25-1160a9. For an excellent and succinct articulation of this point, see John Cooper, "Aristotle on the Forms of Friendship," *The Review of Metaphysics* 30 (1977): 646-647.
35. For Sokolowski's development of this theme as regards language, presence and absence, see Robert Sokolowski, *Presence and Absence: A Philosophical Investigation of Language and Being* (Bloomington: Indiana University Press, 1978), 23-31.
36. Robert Sokolowski, *Moral Action: A Phenomenological Study* (Bloomington: Indiana University Press, 1985), 54-55.
37. Robert Sokolowski, "Friendship and Moral Action in Aristotle," in *The Journal of Value Inquiry* 35 (2001): 367. See also Robert Sokolowski, "What is Moral Action?" *The New Scholasticism* 63 (1989): 18-37; "Moral Thinking," in *Husserl and the Phenomenological Tradition*, ed. Robert Sokolowski (Washington DC: The Catholic University of America Press, 1988), 235-248. The distinction and interrelation between the material performance and the moral categoriality that informs it does not lead to the conclusion that the moral quality of an action depends solely on our intellectual mode of "taking as." Each material performance, considered in distinction from its receptivity to being informed by moral thinking, has its own end, or *telos*, built into to it, and therefore certain material performances are incompatible with certain attempts to take that material performance as good for another human being. The agent must understand the ends both of the material performances he is performing and the ends of the other realities that he is affecting by his performances, such as the end of the other human beings he will affect by his decisions, in order to virtuously respond to the myriad situations of human life. That is, the moral categoriality of "taking as" must be aligned with the ends of the material performance and the ends of the entities one is affecting by one's actions. The moral categoriality of taking something as good or bad

for someone and, as such, doing it as my good or bad must be textured by the nature of the material performance and the one affected by it. In our example, my moral categoriality is bounded by the nature of pushing and the nature of the human being I plan to push in this situation.

38. *St*, II-II, q. 58, a. 1.
39. See *St*, II-II, q. 58, a. 11.
40. See *NE*, IX.4.
41. *NE*, V.1, 1130a12-15.
42. *NE*, V.1, 1130a1-5.
43. See *Metaphysics*, IX.8.
44. For an interesting and helpful discussion of the relationship between justice and friendship according to Aristotle, see Suzanna Stern-Gillet, *Aristotle's Philosophy of Friendship* (Albany: State University of New York Press, 1995), 147-170.
45. See Robert Sokolowski, "What is Natural Law," 507-529. See also Francis Slade, "Ends and Purposes," in *Final Causality in Nature and Human Affairs*, ed. Richard F. Hassing (Washington DC: The Catholic University of America Press, 1997), 83-85; "On the Ontological Priority of Ends and its Relevance to the Narrative Arts," in *Beauty, Art, and the Polis*, ed. Alice Ramos (Washington DC: The Catholic University of America Press, 2000), 58-69. To define the natural law this way does not conflict with Aquinas's definition of the natural law as "the rational creature's participation in the eternal law." Aquinas's definition is the "real" or "scientific" definition, capturing what is first in the order of being, while Slade and Sokolowski give the "nominal" definition, capturing what is first in the order of discovery. See *St*, I-II, q. 91, a. 2.
46. Robert Sokolowski, "What is Natural Law: Human Purposes and Natural Ends," *The Thomist* 68 (2004): 509.
47. *Politics*, I.2, 1252b30-35.
48. See *NE*, III.2, 1111b19-30.
49. Robert Sokolowski, "Discovery and Obligation in Natural Law," in *Natural Moral Law in Contemporary Society*, ed. Holger Zaborowski (Washington DC: The Catholic University of America Press, 2010), 31.
50. *Ibid.*, 32.
51. See Plato, *Apology*, 17d-18a.
52. See Aristotle, *NE*, V.7, 1134b19-1135a15.
53. Aquinas says, "The virtuous person correctly passes judgment on individual things that pertain to human activity. In each case that which is truly good seems to him to be good. This happens because things seem naturally pleasurable to each habit that are proper to it, that is, agree with it. Those things are agreeable to the habit of virtue that are in truth good because the habit of moral virtue is defined by what is in accord with right reason. Thus the things in accord with right reason, things of themselves good, seem good to it. Here the good man

differs very much indeed from others, for he sees what is truly good in individual practicable matters, being as it were the rule and measure of all that is to be done." Commentary on Aristotle's *Nicomachean Ethics*, Bk. III, Ch. 4, lect. 10, #494, commenting on Aristotle, *NE*, III.4, 1113a20-1113b1.
54. For the connection between natural law and virtue, see *St*, I-II, q. 94, a. 3.
55. See *NE*, III.4, 1113a22-1113b1.
56. Kevin Flannery, *Action and Character According to Aristotle: The Logic of the Moral Life* (Washington, DC: The Catholic University of America Press, 2013), 229.
57. *Politics*, I.1, 1253a30-40; II.4, 1266b32-1267a18.
58. *Politics*, II.7, 1267a6-9.
59. For Aristotle's claim that temperance gets its name (*sōphrosunē*) from the fact that it preserves prudence (*sōzousan tēn phronēsin*), see *NE*, VI.5.
60. See *NE*, V.1, 1129b25-1130a13.
61. See *NE*, VIII.4, 1157a25-29.
62. For discussion of how a politician-legislator brings the *polis* into being, see *Politics* I.2; II.12, 1273b30-34; III.3, 1276b1-11, VII.4, 1325b40-1326a38. Aristotle claims that the *polis* is both natural and brought about by the efficient causality of the legislator. For discussion of these claims and an excellent interpretation of why they are not contradictory or even in tension, see Fred D. Miller, *Nature, Justice, and Rights in Aristotle's Politics* (Oxford: Oxford University Press, 1995), 27-61.
63. See *Politics*, I.2, 1253a30-40; IV.1, 1289a10-20; VII.4, 1326a25-32.
64. See *NE*, VIII.9-11.
65. See *NE*, VIII.11, 1161a10-12.
66. See *NE*, VIII.9, 25-31.
67. See *NE*, VIII.11, 1161a30-35.
68. See *NE*, IX.6, 1167b2-4; *Eudemian Ethics*, 1242a6-8 and 1243a31-b14.
69. See *NE*, IX.10, 1171a14-20.
70. See *NE*, V.1, 1129b12-26; V.2, 1130b20-29; X.9, 1179b20-1180a25; *Politics*, II.7, 1266b30-38.
71. For Aristotle's remarks concerning the natural love and goodwill that exists between human beings, see *NE*, VIII.1, 1155a15-25; IX.5, 1166b29-34.
72. See *St*, I-II, q. 99, a. 1, ad. 2.
73. I wish to thank V. Bradley Lewis and John C. McCarthy for helpful comments on an earlier version of this essay. I also wish to thank Stephen Brock, Russell Hittinger, and Robert Sokolowski for many insightful philosophical conversations about the topics discussed in these pages. Finally, I thank two anonymous reviewers for excellent suggestions that enabled me to improve the structure of this article.

On An Alleged Tension in the *Catechism of the Catholic Church*

Christopher Tollefsen

Recent years have seen an increased interest in questions concerning non-human animals among Catholic thinkers. Charles Camosy, John Berkman, and Celia Deane-Drummond, among others, have argued for the need to rethink the relationship between non-human animals, human persons, God, and creation.[1] They have often constructively but critically drawn on the resources of the Catholic intellectual tradition, such as the works of the Church fathers, of St. Albert and St. Thomas, and even the moral manual tradition.[2] Berkman and Camosy have also drawn particular attention to the treatment of animals in the *Catechism of the Catholic Church* as providing both a resource for thinking about animals, and as a manifestation of a particular tension they see in the Catholic tradition.[3]

Berkman writes of the *Catechism*,

> My summary evaluation of the *Catechism* is that it does not have one clearly consistent view on the moral treatment of non-human animals. Rather, it seems to have a variety of views that are at best in tension with one another, and perhaps even incompatible with each other. While some aspects of the teaching are speciesist, other aspects provide a wonderful starting point for Catholic moral and theological reflection on non-human animals. And still other aspects of it are mystifying, leaving the reader with little guidance on applying the teaching.[4]

Camosy too expresses a mixed judgment about the *Catechism*, identifying with Berkman a number of perceived "tensions" that exist in the space of a mere four sections. Camosy highlights as salutary the *Catechism*'s claim that "we human beings owe non-human animals kindness."[5] He writes, "Very strong language is used. Indeed, it is the language of justice that is used: we owe animals kindness."[6] Yet this stands in contrast with claims that non-human animals may be "used for food and clothing."[7] It also contrasts, in its apparent animal-forward focus, with more anthropocentric claims to the effect that mistreatment of animals is contrary to *human* dignity.[8]

Camosy sees this tension as reflective of a larger tension between two strands of thought in the Catholic tradition, which he names the "Scriptural" position and the "it's all about us" position. According to Camosy, this tension persisted throughout most of the history of the Catholic Church until it was entirely effaced by Vatican II, which came down solidly on the side of "it's all about us." Both Camosy and Berkman see a sort of "lost period" of reflection as the consequence of the Council's treatment, or non-treatment, of animals, in which anthropocentrism and binary thinking were not merely the norm but the unreflective norm for Catholic thinkers, with only a few exceptions. As mentioned, there is now a resurgence of thinking about animals, a resurgence in which the *Catechism* might, however awkwardly, play a helpful role.

The purpose of this paper is to challenge one specific part of the narrative advanced by Camosy and Berkman, namely, their claims about "tensions" in the *Catechism*'s treatment of non-human animals. I think it is possible, desirable, and not terribly difficult to read the *Catechism* as holding a coherent and sensible position on the ontological, moral, and theological status of non-human animals. The key to such a reading is to be guided, in interpreting the *Catechism*, by some important natural law claims that undergird the *Catechism*'s treatment of animals, particularly claims about human dignity, justice, property, and objective goodness. When guided by these claims, it is possible to avoid the "inflationary" readings favored by Berkman and, especially, Camosy, of certain claims made by the *Catechism*. When such readings are avoided, we will see that the *Catechism* does indeed present helpful, albeit compressed, guidance for thinking about our relationships to other animals.

The Tension

Let me begin by identifying more clearly the source of tension that is seen by Camosy and Berkman in the *Catechism*. For Camosy, a deep source of the tension, and also potential fruitfulness, of the *Catechism*'s treatment comes in the claim that "Animals are God's creatures. He surrounds them with his providential care. By their mere existence they bless him and give him glory. Thus men owe them kindness."[9] Camosy connects this claim to the Scriptural view that from the outset of the Bible, "we learn that animals were created 'good,' period. Their value comes from God creating them as the kinds of things that they are, not from their usefulness to human beings."[10] It is true, he acknowledges, that man is given dominion over the rest of the animals. But that dominion, Camosy holds, must be interpreted as the "kind of dominion and rule through the Lordship of Jesus Christ, a dominion characterized by servanthood, self-emptying, and sacrifice."[11]

This conception of dominion is contrasted with one which sees our relationship to non-human creation as a "license to dominate and exploit." This view Camosy associates with the "it's all about us" position, which he believes emerged both from the self-interest of its defenders, and from Platonist, Gnostic, and Stoic intellectual sources. Camosy writes that "[t]his tension between Scripture and the 'it's all about us' position, however, would come to dominate much of the tradition."[12] But the tension—creative or otherwise—is vitiated, argues Camosy, by the Second Vatican Council's relentless anthropocentrism, manifest in the following quotation: "According to the almost unanimous opinion of believers and unbelievers alike, all things on earth should be related to man as their center and crown."[13] Camosy denies that this claim characterizes the Catholic tradition, and concludes, "After Vatican II, we have a collapse of the tension in favor of the 'it's all about us' position. As Berkman laments, moral theologians after the Council—even those interested in ecology and care for creation more broadly—'ignored both the general issue of human responsibilities to non-human animals, and the specific issue of animal cruelty.'"[14]

Why see the claims of the Council as in tension with the claim of the *Catechism* highlighted by Camosy, that we owe animals kindness, and the claim of *Genesis* that God saw that His creation was good? An important part of the answer, I believe, must be found in Camosy's interpretation of the *Catechism*'s claim as a claim about *justice*. Justice is a strong norm, the heart of which is captured in the Golden Rule that one "do unto others as one would have them do unto oneself," and to "not do unto others as one would not have them do unto oneself." Seeing an issue as one of justice *to another* thus requires that one accept the following claims.

First, what is owed in justice must be a matter of obligation: one must do such and such, or avoid such and such. Second, the focus of justice is on its recipient: one's concern in doing justice to another must be that the other gets what is owed to that other. And third, central to the idea of justice is the notion of equality. The Golden Rule makes this clear: treating another as one would be treated oneself is only possible if one sees in the other that which makes one's self worthy of the treatment one expects. Thus, embedded in claims of justice are claims of equality that generate other-focused obligations.

Camosy accepts the first two of these claims as applicable to our animal-related obligations. He finds indications of the other-focused nature of justice in his oft-cited passage from *Genesis*. God's creation, including the creation of animals, is itself good, and that goodness is thus the source of our obligations to that creation. This line of thinking comes to a head in Camosy's claim that our stewardship and dominion over the animals must be modeled on Christ's dominion, with its emphasis on "servanthood, self-emptying, and sacrifice."[15] Acts of self-sacrifice and self-emptying fail to have their meaning if they are pursued instrumentally for the sake of the one making the sacrifice. From the sacrifice of animals for the sake of crops, to the sacrifices made by a parent for her child, the risk in sacrifice is that ultimately it will be pursued not for the sake of the other for whom the sacrifice is made, but as part of an instrumentalizing of that other for the benefit of the "sacrificer." A suggestion of this risk is present in "I desire mercy, not sacrifice." For mercy is undertaken, given, and offered for the sake of bringing good out of an evil another is suffering for that other's sake. There is again no mercy if offered for the aggrandizement of the merciful, or indeed if it is instrumentalized to serve any other set of purposes. So Camosy sees strong obligations of service towards animals as what is owed *to them* in justice.

All this is deeply at odds with the other set of claims Camosy (and Berkman) highlight, however. If "it's all about us" understands dominion as license to exploit, and the Council's claim that man is the center and crown of creation is an "all about us" claim, then the Council is offering a license to exploit. And if eating meat because one enjoys the taste, and perhaps even eating meat at all, is a form of exploitation, then the *Catechism*'s countenancing of the use of animals for food and clothing licenses a form of exploitation. And indeed, it seems that for Camosy this must be true because using something for food or clothing seems to go "beyond caring for the well-being and flourishing of such animals."[16] It is incompatible with a demand for a Christ-like self-emptying servanthood directed *towards* non-human animals. So there really is an unredeemable tension to the extent that the language of "owing" is given a strong "justice-based" interpretation, and to the extent that "dominion" and "care" are interpreted in a Christ-like sense.

Before closing this section, I should comment on an earlier exchange that I have had with Camosy on these issues.[17] In that exchange I also pointed out that Camosy's claims about justice-based obligation in the *Catechism* committed him to claims of equality between those who owe obligations in justice and those to whom the obligations are owed. Camosy responded by denying that he held that there is equality between human and non-human animals, and denying further that they are owed equal treatment. Camosy wrote: "I claim that justice consists in 'being consistent and impartial in giving both individuals and groups what they are owed.' But a relationship of justice in this broad sense can most certainly exist between unequal beings."[18] As I will show below, there are extended senses of justice in relation to which such claims have a certain truth. But, as I shall also show below, in these extended senses, not just animals, but *everything* can be said to be "owed" the appropriate treatment; so this move of Camosy's threatens to evacuate his justice claims of importance.

My own view is that the *Catechism* is using such an extended sense of the "language of justice" when it speaks of "owing" animals certain treatment; the inequality of humans and non-human animals means that there is no justice between them, strictly speaking. But in the earlier exchange, Camosy denied that the *Catechism* could be read in this way: "The verb 'to owe' is not used by the Church to refer to the moral duties we have to creation, broadly speaking."[19] Hence, "mistreatment of plants would not mean the plants had been treated unjustly." In other words, the *Catechism* reserves the language of justice, on Camosy's account, to situations of strict justice; therefore, when it uses the language of justice with regards to animals, we are to take the obligations there too as obligations in strict justice to the animals, the radical inequality between humans and animals notwithstanding.

How to Read the *Catechism*'s Claims

However, these strong, and I would say inflationary, readings of the *Catechism* are uncalled for. A milder reading is possible and warranted, one which is more sensitive to the nuances of moral language and to justice as understood within the natural law tradition. In this section, I provide such a reading; in the next, I address some possible objections.

Let us start with the assertion that the *Catechism* makes a claim of justice on human animals in their treatment of non-human animals. Of course, put simply as I have just put it, this claim is true, and characterizes both traditional Catholic teaching and the natural law thought of St. Thomas Aquinas: some of the obligations we have towards animals are indeed obligations of justice, as are obligations in regards to property more generally. Indeed, we should note that the discussion of animals occurs in the context of a discussion of the Seventh Commandment in the *Catechism*, the commandment prohibiting theft, a norm generated by considerations of justice in regard to property.

Yet the *Catechism*'s treatment of our obligations in this section generally is focused rather obviously not on the rights of property but of persons. The *Catechism*'s view of the goods of the earth, including non-human animals, is that all exist for the benefit of human beings. The *Catechism* begins its treatment of the Seventh Commandment with this claim: "The goods of creation are destined for the whole human race."[20] In this, the *Catechism* follows Aquinas's treatment of the matter, and for similar reasons: only man is made to "the image and likeness of God," i.e., possessing freedom and reason. This ontological fact about human beings' nature, which is also the source of the radical inequality between human and non-human animals, is, for Aquinas, the reason for human dominion over the rest of the natural world, including the other animals.

Although the goods of the earth exist for the good of all human persons, Aquinas argues that the division of those goods into private property is justified and entitles individuals to exercise personal authority over their goods. But as to use, Aquinas says, that should be in common, i.e., for the sake of the common good. Failures to respect private property, as well as failures to use private property in ways that contribute to the common good, are thus both failures of justice as it regards other human persons.[21] The *Catechism* follows Aquinas in these points: it asserts in 2402 that the goods of the earth are rightly divided up, but in 2403 asserts that nevertheless the universal destination of the world's goods "remains primordial."

Since non-human animals are among the goods of creation, there can thus be failures of justice also with regard to those animals. Theft of another's cow is unjust and so is wasteful treatment of animals, such as failing to make use of labor animals one owns when others need that labor, or the lavishing of personal resources on a pet when those resources could better be used charitably to relieve other person's needs (a point made in section 2418). If human beings benefit from the existence of a species, such as the American bison, then the elimination of that species without good reason likewise constitutes an offense against justice–to those human beings who will now not receive the benefit.[22]

Of course, as Camosy, St. Thomas, and the *Catechism* recognize, the special nature of non-human animals means that our treatment of them cannot be exactly like our treatment of other forms of property. Animals are, unlike fields or plows, living; they can experience pain and something similar to suffering, although their experience of suffering cannot be said to be unqualifiedly like ours, and is, I believe, called "suffering" only by analogy.[23] Because of our physical kinship with animals, and because they are objectively higher forms of creation than both plants and inanimate matter, we must be sensitive to these differences between non-human animals and the rest of sub-personal nature, avoiding the infliction of pain and relieving their quasi–forms of suffering when possible, and treating animals in ways that, again because of our physical kinship with them, will conduce to virtuous treatment of other human beings. We should thus not be cruel, and should treat them with kindness.[24]

Now the argument of the previous paragraph is rooted in the natural law and concludes with an obligation to act in a certain way—with kindness—but which makes no claims to rights to such treatment on the part of animals, and no claims to the effect that the obligation is an obligation *in justice* to the animals in question. It is, I think, the argument that stands behind the *Catechism*'s claims, since it is for the most part the argument made by those figures such as Aquinas who are the sources for the *Catechism*'s treatment. Can the conclusion of such an argument be put in the way the *Catechism* puts its claims without requiring the stronger reading offered by Camosy? I believe so.

Note first that the *Catechism* says neither that animals *have* a right to this kindness, nor even that they are owed the kindness. We owe it, and of course they are the recipients of that kindness. So one might say, as the *Catechism* does, "we owe them kindness," without this being either a rights claim or a (paradigmatic) justice claim in regards to the animals. This form of speech is not unusual: "That is your father's (car, tie, book, pipe, etc.), and you owe it better treatment than that" manifests the same pattern and does not imply that the *object* is owed the treatment.

Indeed, the whole range of words that are used in this discussion—owes, justice, respect —are words with a wide range of analogous meanings, not univocal to their use in their paradigm cases. In the paradigm case, what one owes to another is owed in justice, and giving what one owes, or what is due, is a matter of showing appropriate respect to that other within a frame of equality. In the paradigm case, the respect owed in justice is the respect owed to persons; and the showing of that respect manifests one's recognition of the equal dignity of those persons, the special, indeed, unique, excellence of those members of creation that are both rational and free; it is the equality of this dignity that sets the frame of equality within which justice in the paradigm sense is discerned and done.

But one can be said to "owe respect" to many things that are not persons, and in giving that respect, one can be said to have done justice to those things. This Rembrandt painting is beautiful, but is neither a person nor possessed of dignity; yet one can be said to owe it certain forms of treatment, and when one fails to give it that treatment, mishandling it, perhaps, one can be told "Respect the Rembrandt!"

Indeed, of *everything* it can be said that we should respect what it is, and thus that we owe it this or that form of treatment (or that this treatment is "due" to it). It can further be said that in so acting we "do justice to" whatever it is that is under consideration. Thus, "It is delicate, and we owe it gentle treatment"; "respect its delicate nature"; and "this does not do justice to its delicate quality" are all acceptable renderings of the ordinary obligation to treat things in accordance with their natures. Aquinas makes a similar point in considering whether there is justice in God, for he identifies a form of justice present in treating something—anything — as it ought to be treated, and God manifests this form of justice in his relations with *all* of creation. Thus Aquinas quotes Dionysius: "God is truly just, [in that] He gives to all existing things what is proper to the condition of each."[25]

It is in this sense that the claim that we owe animals kindness should also be construed. The claim simply does not automatically imply that we are talking about justice in what I have called its paradigm sense; nor can a claim which is true about everything be said, *pace* Camosy, to be "very strong language." It is a true, but weak, claim, which is consistent with the natural law view that animals, being non-persons, and thus without the dignity of persons, and thus radically unequal to us, have no rights of the sort that are the object of giving justice to another. By contrast, Camosy's "strong" reading is incompatible with the ontological differences between humans and other animals, and is inconsistent with almost everything else said by the *Catechism* about those animals.

So, while it is not incorrect that what is owed is determined (in part, at least) by the nature of what we are talking about—and thus, that animals are to receive different treatment than fields and plows—it is an error to think that this "owing" is the owing of justice in anything but an extended sense. There is thus no justice *between* human beings and the other animals, nor is any implied by the *Catechism*'s choice of words. Rather, the absence of such a relationship between humans and the other animals is the clear implication of the decision to place treatment of animals within the larger treatment of property and the goods of the earth, to say nothing of the *Catechism*'s repeated statements that animals exist for the sake of human beings.[26]

What of the claim that only non-human animals are singled out as owed certain forms of treatment, and that therefore we should read "owes" in the *Catechism* as having a sense univocal to its use in paradigmatic expressions about justice to human beings? Here, I think, we must look at the initial framing of the discussion of non-human animals, which reflects much of my discussion so far. The *Catechism* begins its discussion of non-human animals under the heading "Respect for the integrity of creation." It continues:

> The seventh commandment enjoins respect for the integrity of creation. Animals, like plants and inanimate beings, are by nature destined for the common good of past, present, and future humanity. Use of the mineral, vegetable, and animal resources of the universe cannot be divorced from respect for moral imperatives. Man's dominion over inanimate and other living beings granted by the Creator is not absolute; it is limited by concern for the quality of life of his neighbor, including generations to come; it requires a religious respect for the integrity of creation.[27]

There are several points to be made about this passage. First, the "language of justice" is present right from the outset in the phrase "respect for the integrity of creation," a phrase found both in the title and in the content of the section. But this "respect" clearly encompasses non-animal aspects of creation. Or consider the claim that our treatment of minerals and vegetables is not divorced from moral imperatives. One might infer from these claims that creation is owed respectful treatment in justice, both as to animate *and inanimate* things. But this would be inflationary, as we see from the end. There, the *Catechism* provides the justification for why the integrity of all creation requires respect. That justification follows the traditional direction of natural law thought: our obligations in regards to all creation stem from concern for other human persons, who must not be denied their opportunity to enjoy the gifts of creation, and to God, to whom we show lack of gratitude, *inter alia*, in failing to respect the integrity of all His creation.

The structure of the *Catechism*'s treatment here is important. It begins with the moral obligations we have in respect of all creation, and the reasons underlying those obligations. Those obligations are justice obligations, though it would be an error to infer from this that we therefore have obligations in justice to, say, the Grand Canyon. The *Catechism* then goes on, as I have done, to identify the morally relevant ways in which living beings differ from the rest of creation; as *creatures*, that is, as living beings, they can be misused in ways that rock formations and plants, for example, cannot be: they can be treated cruelly or caused to suffer unnecessarily.

And this should not be done, because, as the *Catechism* notes, to do so is contrary to our human dignity.

There is one final point to make about the language of "justice" as it is used to describe our obligations in regards to creation quite generally. The second citation of section 2415 is to St. John Paul II's *Centessimus Annus*, sections 37-38. That discussion of John Paul's Encyclical concerns the "ecological question" raised by man's "senseless destruction of the natural environment." Here the Pope does not single animals out for additional treatment but instead addresses the tendency of man to subject all things to his "arbitrary" will; man's consumption is described as "excessive" and "disordered" and his attitude as divorced from truth. Here too the "language of justice" is used very broadly. But here too, at the end of the discussion, the Pope comes back to the two central problems with such attitudes: a failure to relate properly to God through His creation, and a failure to respect "duties and obligations towards future generations."

I conclude that in its treatment of what is "owed" in respect to God's creation, no special use of justice terms can be identified in regards to animals that either is not or could not be used to characterize our obligations in regards to creation more generally. What we do find are special obligations in regards to animals deriving from the differences in animal nature from the nature of all sub-animal creation. Those differences are relevant for us, in our observance of our obligations. But they do not generate obligations of justice to those animals, nor can animals be said, as the recipients of justice-based obligations can be said, to possess rights to those forms of treatment.

I turn now to the use of the language of "dominion" and "stewardship." Here too one must recognize a multiplicity of senses. I will focus on the former, for it will allow me to make an important point about the role of animals in God's creation and in human lives.

It is clear that dominion has multiple senses. Aquinas himself distinguishes between the dominion of a master over a slave, and the dominion of a ruler over free men, and argues that the latter was appropriate to relationships among pre-fallen men while the former was not.[28] What is characteristic of the second sense of dominion is that it is exercised, as Aquinas says, for the good of those over whom it is exercised or for the common good. It is not exercised for the benefit of the one exercising dominion.

Now human beings are said to have dominion over the animals, and indeed over all creation. Is this claim a claim of the first or second sort of dominion? I believe it is a claim that straddles the two senses. The dominion in question *is* to be exercised for the common good, and not simply for personal gain.[29] Moreover, the well-being of animals is in a sense included in that common good, as I will show shortly. But animals are not ruled as free persons (a claim that I believe my interlocutors also accept). Their relationship to the common good is thus not that of the persons for whose sake authority is exercised; animals cannot be part of the common good in that way. But animal existence can and ought to serve the common good, and humans rightly exercise dominion over animals when their treatment of animals serves the common good of human persons. This point is made, as I have noted, by the *Catechism* about the world's goods generally, and likewise by the Second Vatican Council. It is also made by Aquinas, and is a characteristic claim of the natural law tradition.

Now, in opposition to this, Camosy claims that the good of animals is to be served in the exercise of dominion over them. And Camosy believes that this service to the good of animals is incompatible—or at least in tension with—treatment of animals as fundamentally for the sake of human beings, as using animals for food and clothing surely does treat them. But again, I think the tension is illusory. For if animals are, as the *Catechism* holds, made by God for the sake of human beings, then using animals in ways that benefit the common good of human beings is precisely acting in a way that serves the good of animals—it achieves the purposes for which animal creation exists. So there is a way in which Camosy's claims about the need for human actions to serve the good of animals is, in fact, true.

I should note two qualifications here. The first is that not every purpose for which we may use animals is morally legitimate. Camosy frequently obscures this point by describing the dominion/it's all about us position into which he thinks Vatican II stumbled as licensing the more or less indiscriminate "exploitation" of animals for whatever we desire. That also is an inflationary claim and does not reflect the natural law tradition. Many are the purposes that men could make animals to serve that would be immoral: as weapons of an unjust war, for example, were rats infected with plague and catapulted into a besieged city; or as objects of scorn and cruel mockery, were the feathers to be plucked from a bird for sport. But no natural law thinker would ever license such acts, for the natural law tradition simply does not assume that all purposes are equally acceptable. Rather, purposes not ratified by human nature, as known through practical reason, are not to be done and pursued. It follows that when the use of animals is not fundamentally in accord with reason and virtue, then they are not being used in ways that serve the common good of human persons, or in ways that serve their own good.

Second, the purposes in question are not exhausted by our needs for food and clothing. There are clearly other purposes which are served by the presence of the non-human animals among us, including the vast aesthetic value of creation; the epistemic value of creation (as Thomas says, the animals were necessary to pre-fallen men for the sake of knowledge); the religious purposes of creation; and so on. But it is easy to make the following error: because maintaining animals in existence for the sake of their aesthetic value does not, while eating animals does, result in the loss of an animal's life, one might conclude that only the latter form of treatment "makes use" of animals, or shows dominion, and likewise that only the former form of treatment involves treatment that is for the good of the animals. Rather, we need to see that in both forms of treatment animals are treated as serving human purposes and are therefore treated in ways that serve their genuine good. There are, however, important distinctions here that I will address in the next section.

Objections

In this section, I will address two possible objections to the claims I have just made. The first is that my claim that animals exist for the sake of human persons is incompatible with the view that animals have value for their own sake. Since both claims seem to be endorsed by the *Catechism*, their compatibility or not is essential to determining whether the *Catechism* manifests internal tensions.

The second, more targeted, objection is that animals were not created for human use as food, as indicated by the "vegetarian" diet given to pre-fallen man. Camosy holds that "It is only after sin that God first gives human beings limited permission to kill and eat animals."[30] And he then asks "Why, then, do so many claim that animals were created by God for our use and exploitation?"[31] Leaving aside the conflation of use and exploitation, the objection might be put in this way: the "use" that the *Catechism* licenses us to make of animals is only a postlapsarian concession to sin, and not that to which human-animal relations were originally called. On its surface, this objection asserts that the *Catechism* (and St. Thomas) is guilty of a straightforward error when it holds that "Animals, like plants and inanimate beings, are by nature destined for the common good of past, present, and future humanity."[32] Of course, error is in tension with truth, so if false, this claim is in tension with any true claims the *Catechism* makes about animals.

On, then, to the first objection, that one cannot say both that animals have value for themselves, and that they exist and are created for the good of human beings. Camosy is led into difficulty here in part because his value taxonomy seems to encompass only two mutually exclusive categories. On the one hand, there is that which has value for its own sake; on the other, there is that which may be used (exploited) for the sake of another and which therefore receives its value from the other's purposes. We could say of the former category that entities within this category have intrinsic value. It is clear that animals really do have such value. Their value is not extrinsic: they do not get value (or *all* their value) from the fact that human beings are able to use them as resources. In this they are unlike, e.g., money, which receives its value from its relationship to human purposes and indeed from human beings valuing it. Of money, it seems entirely reasonable to say that its meaning is exhausted by whatever use we human beings make of it; of animals, it does not seem reasonable.

But there are problems with this stark (binary!) distinction. To begin with, not everything that can be used instrumentally has only instrumental value: many, if not all, basic goods, such as knowledge or health, can also be used instrumentally. So having instrumental value in some respects does not mean having only extrinsic value. Second, within the category of intrinsic value there are reasons to make some further distinctions. For example, animals do not have the kind of intrinsic value that basic goods have, since they are not basic reasons for action capable of motivating human beings in virtue of their offering benefits constitutive of human well-being. Nor do they have the intrinsic value of persons: they do not have the kind of dignity that human beings possess in virtue of their freedom and reason which puts them, as Kant would say, beyond price. Thus not everything of intrinsic value is of equal value or the same kind of value.

Clearly, the category of that which has intrinsic value is rather wide. The *Mona Lisa* is neither a person nor a basic good, but it also does not have its value entirely by virtue of human beings valuing it, strictly extrinsically. And while its value is tied up with human purposes—it has value as a work of beauty, and thus as something that can be a source of our experience of the basic good of aesthetic enjoyment—at the same time it makes good sense to say that this work of art has intrinsic value. Its value is objective, not endowed or bestowed on it, and its place in the economy of human choices, including the choice to enjoy its beauty, is normatively determined by its intrinsic properties, and not merely by those human choices.

I believe that is an important category of entities with intrinsic value: things that are objectively beautiful. The appreciation of the beauty of such entities is a basic good. Now, given that aesthetic enjoyment is a basic good, and one served by entities that have objective aesthetic value themselves, then had God wanted to create a world for human persons in which there was to be aesthetic value for those persons, then He would have needed to create a world in which aesthetic value was there in the world for human beings. And the realities possessed of that aesthetic value would themselves have intrinsic, and not merely extrinsic or bestowed, value. Had God desired this state of affairs, He would have created beings of which it was true both that they were good (although we could say of their goodness that it was, among other forms of goodness, aesthetic goodness, the goodness of beauty) and that they were destined for the common good of human beings.

But these claims do indeed seem to be true of the world that God created: its beauty is intrinsically good, and that intrinsic goodness is compatible with its having been created for human beings. In other words, there is nothing paradoxical in holding that God created, *inter alia*, animals with intrinsic value—good, period—for the sake of human persons. (Think of what our world would be like if everything non-human only had extrinsic value!). This thought seems to have been centrally motivating for John Paul II in his concern for the ecological question:

> In all this, one notes first the poverty or narrowness of man's outlook, motivated as he is by a desire to possess things rather than to relate them to the truth, and lacking that disinterested, unselfish and aesthetic attitude that is born of wonder in the presence of being and of the beauty which enables one to see in visible things the message of the invisible God who created them.[33]

So even while manifesting the goodness they have in themselves, animals can serve (and even exist for) human purposes. Is the intrinsic goodness of animals limited to their aesthetic goodness? I think the answer is no; I have already identified epistemic and religious purposes as also aspects of the intrinsic goodness of animals. But neither are the ways that animals are legitimately of use to us limited to enjoyment of their intrinsic goodness; making this point will eventually carry us to the second objection.

Suppose that, as I have argued, animals have intrinsic goodness and are created for the sake of human beings. That intrinsic goodness includes their aesthetic value, which is thus rightly enjoyed by human beings; it likely includes other values as well. Does all this require that the proper use of animals be limited only to that about animals that manifests that intrinsic goodness? If so, this might imply the kind of protectionist approach advocated by Camosy and Berkman, though not for quite the same reasons. One could hold on this view that animals were not to be killed for meat, for example, because this was not in keeping with the enjoyment of animals' intrinsic value; but one would not be committed by this view to the claims that human beings are not the crown of creation, nor the claim that animals were not created for the sake of the human common good.

I do not think we should accept this view. Not all the ways in which animals serve human purposes are or must be related to the ways in which they have intrinsic value. That the hides of some animals are especially conducive to keeping human beings warm is, I think, accidental to the nature of an animal, and hence to its intrinsic goodness. But it is very important to human beings. So to the extent that animals are generally given over to humans to serve their purposes, to that extent they may be used for their hides. Likewise, both the nourishment that some animal flesh can provide, and the enjoyment that its taste can provide, are accidental to the nature of animals. They are not reflections of the intrinsic goodness of animals. Nevertheless, to the extent that animals are created and given over to the service of human purposes, to that extent they can be used for food, both nourishing and tasty. Unlike the enjoyment of animals for their natural beauty, such eating does not quite, I think, manifest an appreciation of the intrinsic goodness of animals; but it is nevertheless compatible with that value if animals are created under the dominion of human beings as I described that dominion above. Use of animals in those respects in which they are accidentally useful would not vitiate the claim that such animals also possess intrinsic value.

Moreover, we should recall an earlier claim I made. If created under human dominion, for the sake of the human common good, then even those human appropriations of animals that are not strictly appreciations of the intrinsic goodness of animals, such as eating and wearing animals and use of their derivate products, nevertheless can be carried out in a way that is for the good of the animals themselves; for God's creation of the animals for human purposes was not limited to only those purposes that were served by the intrinsic value of animals.

Or was it? It is a part of the narrative advanced by Camosy, and also Berkman, that the permission given for the eating of animals is a consequence of the fall. If this is so, then there might well be an important difference between the enjoyment of animals in their beauty, and the enjoyment of animals on the plate. The former might be, while the latter is not, true to the original purposes of animals. Are Camosy and Berkman correct in their assessment? Were this the case, the argument against eating animals would not be definitive, since permission clearly was granted; but it would be weakened at least for those striving to live as Godly a life as they could.

Aquinas, at any rate, would not have agreed with Camosy or Berkman; while I do not assert the view on his authority, nevertheless, it gives some weight to the counter view—enough, I think, to dissolve quick claims of incoherence or tension in the *Catechism*. For the *Catechism* is probably holding something like Aquinas's own view. And Aquinas's view has its own merits, which I shall try to identify.

Aquinas's view is that the animals are created for the sake of human beings, for their use; this is Aquinas's understanding of the mastership that men have over animals.[34] As he says, "the imperfect are for the use of the [more] perfect," and "therefore, it is in keeping with the order of nature, that man should be master over the animals."[35] Of course, use is a correlative notion to *need*, an important concept for determining the proper moral limits of our treatment of animals. Animals are not just for any purpose that man could devise; rather, mastery extends over those uses that answer to human needs.[36]

And this is why, for Aquinas, three uses were not made of animals in the Garden: for clothing, for food, and for carriage. Use was not made of animals in these respects because there were no human needs to which such uses could answer. There was no need of the first because human beings were naked but not ashamed; there was no need of the second because humans fed on the trees of paradise; and there was no need of the third because human bodies were sufficiently strong for that purpose. But, says Aquinas, "man needed animals in order to have experimental knowledge of their natures. This is signified by the fact that God led the animals to man, that he might give them names expressive of their respective natures."[37] Note that we have here something like the distinction I drew above: man's needs in the Garden with respect to animals are satisfied by aspects of the animals' intrinsic nature and goodness, in this case as objects of knowledge (their being, which is the object of knowledge, is itself intrinsically good). Aquinas does not mention the beauty of animals, but I see no reason to think he would deny that. But Aquinas does not think that the various accidental purposes to which animals may be put were relevant to man in the unfallen state.

Now this claim might seem like a concession to which the defender of animals will have two points to make in reply. First the defender might say, yes, well, is there truly any such need now? Cannot human beings, or at least many human beings, obtain what they need without killing and eating animals? If so, should they not do so? And second, to repeat the starting point of the objection, is not the permission to eat not merely a consequence of, but a concession to human sinfulness and fallenness, and not what God originally intended vis-à-vis animal-human relationships? Indeed, Camosy goes so far as to say that "According to the creation story, God's original creation is a place of deathless non-violence" in which both human and non-human animals are vegetarians.[38]

Let us start with the second point. What does it mean to ascribe man's needs in these respects to the fall? And is there a more broken quality to the cosmos that brings animal killing and eating with it after the fall, even to the other animals? Again, Aquinas does not think so. He mentions the opinion of some that fierce animals would have been tame in regards to one another before the fall, and not only in regards to man, and rejects this as "quite unreasonable. For the nature of animals was not changed by man's sin, as if those whose nature now it is to devour the flesh of others, would then have lived on herbs."[39] There existed, then, a pattern of animals eating animals before the fall; that pattern did not begin with man's sinfulness. And nothing in the nature of the animals changed after the fall that would have led to the permission to eat them.

Is the eating of animals a concession to sin in the way that multiple marriage and divorce were concessions that Moses allowed? There is no suggestion in Aquinas that this is the case. And the early Christian tradition is more permissive than the Jewish tradition where meat-eating is concerned, not less.[40] So the question remains, what did change that led to humans eating animals? The simple answer is that the scope of human needs grew upon expulsion from the Garden. That for which there was once no need now became needful, and because the permitted scope of the use of animals was universal over all legitimate needs of human beings, it merely became the case that now animals were legitimately used to serve more needs than they once were.

This leads to the first objection, however. Is the scope of our needs still the same, or can we not accommodate our needs without making use of animals, especially our need for food and clothing, just as most of us no longer make our way on the backs of animals, but instead use the products of human manufacture?

I think that this argument, like many considered already, relies upon too strong an understanding of one of the crucial terms, in this case "need." Is the kind of need for which we can make use of animals linked to the absolute necessity that something must have for our survival or welfare? On such a reading, if we could survive without eating animals, we should. Likewise, if we could make medical progress without experimenting upon them, engage in sport without hunting them, and dress ourselves without wearing them, we should. But I suggest that the index of need, from which derives the scope of permissible use, is not bare exigency but rather what was lost upon expulsion from the Garden.

And what was lost? Clearly, a source of nourishment, and our ability modestly to go without clothes. Human health was lost, as indicated by Aquinas's remarks on the need to now make use of animals for carriage. So the use of animals for nourishment, clothes, and health is justified. Here we see, I believe, the deep justification for experimentation on animals. But was nourishment the only food-related good lost when man was banished from Eden? Surely not: the fruits of the trees in the garden must have been delicious beyond almost any earthly reckoning.[41] And so an understanding of what was lost in terms of food must go beyond a loss of the merely nutritive.

If we take this route, then I think it is open to us to say that the scope of our need includes the variety of taste, texture, and culinary opportunity provided by fish, fowl, and animal. If one is satisfied, of course, with a vegan, vegetarian, pescatarian, or other diet, then one has no obligation to make use of animals as food. But many people find the flesh of fish, fowl, and animals not only satisfying, but, as it were, a palette on which creatively to engage with their food in skilled ways, in the raising, hunting, butchering, cooking, presenting, and eating of them. It seems to me that there is no way in which these individuals can be said to be falling short of a moral ideal; rather, many of them create food that, although perhaps only a pale imitation of what was lost, nevertheless are anticipations of the heavenly banquet to which we look forward.

My discussion here barely even scratches the surface of what a full discussion of the goods of food (and drink!) would have to engage with, and says nothing about what standards of care our raising, hunting, killing, cooking, serving, and eating of animals should meet, though this is an important topic. But I hope it is suggestive. There are, as implied by what I have said here, and said more explicitly elsewhere, good reasons to be concerned about factory farming and our general approach to food; there are good reasons as well to be concerned about our disposable, wasteful, unskilled treatment of meat in our home kitchens. But those reasons do not trade on arguments about justice to animals or their rights; nor do they concede that our eating of animals is a concession to human sinfulness. Indeed, my point here is that, rather than a concession, our eating of animals in a way is almost the opposite. It is a substitution; God's permission to humans to eat animals was itself a mercy, bestowed by a creator who was mindful of just how much had been lost by our expulsion from the Garden of Earthly Delights.

Conclusion

Camosy's and Berkman's readings of the *Catechism of the Catholic Church* lead them to claim that that document, in its treatment of non-human animals, suffers from internal tensions and conflicts, perhaps even contradictions. But if one reads those sections with sensitivity to the ways in which the "language of justice" is a language of analogy, with sensitivity to the ways in which the *Catechism*'s treatment of animals is situated within a larger discussion of justice and the world's natural goods, and with sensitivity to the natural law thought of one of the *Catechism*'s main sources, St. Thomas Aquinas, then I think the appearance of tension is dissolved entirely. Instead, we are left with a nuanced position, entirely justified on natural law grounds, that attributes intrinsic value to animals but no rights; that acknowledges limits to the justified forms of treatment of animals by human persons, but no obligations in justice to those animals; and that sees a generous range of ways in which humans can use other animals for the common good that are also for the good of those animals, even when those uses result in the animals' deaths. These contrasting claims can seem starkly incoherent if severed from the tradition of natural law thought within which they are embedded. But when viewed within the broader framework of that tradition, I believe they are coherent, defensible, and, indeed, true.

Notes

1. See, e.g., Charles Camosy, *For Love of Animals: Christian Ethics, Consistent Action*. Franciscan Media, 2013; see also the special issue of the *Journal of Moral Theology* 3, 2014, ed. by John Berkman, Charles Camosy, and Celia Deane-Drummond, and Celia Deane-Drummond and David Clough, *Creaturely Theology: On God, Humans and Other Animals*. (London: SCM Press, 2009).
2. See John Berkman, "From Theological Speciesism to a Theological Ethology: Where Catholic Moral Theology Needs to Go," *Journal of Moral Theology* 3, 2014, 11-34.
3. In addition to Berkman, op. cit., see Charles Camosy, "Locating *Laudato Si'* Along a Catholic Trajectory of Concern for Non-Human Animals," *Lex Naturalis* 2, 2016, 1-20.
4. Berkman, "From Theological Speciesm to a Theological Ethology," 25.
5. *Catechism of the Catholic Church*, 2nd ed. New York: Doubleday, 2003, no. 2416.
6. Camosy, "Locating *Laudato Si,*" 8.
7. *Catechism of the Catholic Church*, no. 2417.
8. *Ibid*., no. 2418.
9. *Ibid*., no. 2416.
10. Camosy, "Locating *Laudato Si,*" 4.
11. *Ibid*.
12. *Ibid*., p. 5.
13. "Pastoral Constitution on the Church in the Modern World, Gaudium et Spes" Promulgated by His Holiness Pope Paul VI, December 7, 1965, no. 12.
14. Camosy, "Locating *Laudato Si,*" 6-7.
15. It is also apparent in his frequent references to the "vulnerable" status of animals.
16. Camosy, "Locating *Laudato Si,*" 8.
17. The exchange began with my two-part review of his book: Christopher Tollefsen, "What Our Obligations to Animals Are Not," Public Discourse December 19, 2013. On-Line: http://www.thepublicdiscourse.com/2013/12/11730/; and "Our Obligations To Animals," Public Discourse December 20, 2013.
18. Charles Camosy, "What We Owe Animals: A Response to Christopher Tollefsen," Public Discourse February 24, 2014. On-line: http://www.thepublicdiscourse.com/2014/02/12114/.
19. *Ibid*.
20. *Catechism of the Catholic Church*, no. 2402.
21. Aquinas's treatment of these matters is found in the *Summa Theologiae*, II-II, Q. 66, aa. 1-2.
22. The American bison were brought to the point of near extinction in the late nineteenth century, in part because of wasteful hunting by non-indigenous whites.

23. I argue that only rational beings can suffer in the strict sense in Christopher Tollefsen, "Suffering, Enhancement, and Human Goods," *Quaestiones Disputatae* 5, 2015, 104-117.
24. Aquinas interprets some Old Testament ceremonial precepts in this manner, *ST* I-II, Q. 102, a. 6; and he makes the same point in *Summa Contra Gentiles* III, no. 112.
25. *ST* I, Q. 21, a. 1. Aquinas then goes on to say that *ultimately*, the one who is owed in this form of justice is in fact God, because of the ordering of all creation to God: "He himself is not the debtor, since He is not directed to other things, but rather other things to Him" (*Ibid.*, ad. 3). My thanks to an anonymous referee for suggesting this reference.
26. In fact, this claim is, as the passage from Aquinas about God's justice indicates, consistent rather with the view that human beings are not "debtors" in what they owe in regards to animals, but are rather the penultimate objects of the obligation, with God as the final object.
27. *Catechism of the Catholic Church*, no. 2415.
28. *ST*, I, Q. 96, a. 4.
29. Here I think my view is not quite that of Aquinas, who seems to envisage man's dominion over the animals as of the first kind: "every other creature is naturally subject to slavery" (SCG, III, no. 112.).
30. Camosy, "Locating *Laudato Si*,'" 4.
31. *Ibid.*
32. *Catechism of the Catholic Church*, no. 2415.
33. Pope John Paul II, Encyclical Letter *Centesimus Annus*, May I, 1991, no. 37. On-line: http://w2.vatican.va/content/john-paul-ii/en/encyclicals/documents/hf_jp-ii_enc_01051991_centesimus-annus.html.
34. Neither the *Catechism* nor the Second Vatican Council were innovators in making this claim.
35. *ST* I, Q. 96, a1.
36. Thus, what is "needless" forms the limit point at which our treatment of animals is immoral for the *Catechism*; no. 2418. Similarly, we should see the "needful" as providing the boundary conditions for the concept of "cruelty" as applied to our treatment of animals. Within the bounds of the needful, our treatment of animals simply is not cruel. It is therefore an error, both conceptual and exegetical, of Berkman's to say of Germain Grisez's view that he seems to "acknowledge that we should not be cruel to animals without good reason" (Berkman, 2014, p. 23). Rather, Grisez holds (in Germain Grisez, *The Way of Our Lord Jesus*, Vol. 2, *Living a Christian Life* (Chicago: Franciscan, 1993, p. 786) that we should not be cruel to animals for two reasons, viz., that "they are parts of God's good creation," and thus "should not be disturbed without a good reason," since doing so is an irreverence to God; and that causing pain or harm to animals without good reason manifests

either anger, hatred, or a desire to take pleasure in animal suffering, which is contrary to the good of personal integrity; relatedly, such cruelty "often predisposes the agent or others to act cruelly toward people." What are good reasons? The answer again is human need, the "service of human goods." But then treatment of animals in service to the human good is not cruel, even when it causes pain or harm. Grisez's view is thus that one should never be cruel to animals. This is my view as well, and also, I believe, the *Catechism*'s.
37. *Ibid.*, ad. 3.
38. Camosy, "Locating *Laudato Si*,'" 4.
39. Aquinas, *ST* I, Q. 96, a. 1, ad. 2
40. Berkman himself notes that "much of the Catholic tradition" follows Augustine and Aquinas in understanding "St Paul to be denying in principle objections to all consumption of animal flesh" in "The Consumption of Animals and the Catholic Tradition," *Logos* 7, 2004, p, 178. As Berkman points out, this is entirely compatible with being concerned with further questions about when, why, and how one should and should not eat meat.
41. Compare Lewis's treatment of the food in his novel *Perelandra*, which is also delicious in mind-opening ways; the role of food in Lewis's fictional paradise is discussed is Susan J. Navarette, "The Fine Reality of Hunger Satisfied: Food and Desire in C.S. Lewis's *Perelandra*, in Westfahl, Slusser, and Rabkin, eds., *Foods of the Gods: Eating and the Eaten in Fantasy and Science Fiction.* (Athens: University of Georgia Press, 1996), 97-114.

Bartolomé de las Casas and the Long and Very Long, and the Short and Very Short, History of Human Rights

Paul J. Cornish

Prologue

Consider, for instance, the contents of the consciousness of a man who is protesting against injustice, let us say, in a case where his own interests are not touched and where the injustice is wrought by technically correct legislation. The contents of his consciously protesting mind would be something like these. He is asserting that there is an idea of justice; that this idea is transcendent to the actually expressed will of the legislator; that it is rooted somehow in the nature of things; that he really *knows* this idea; that it is not made by his judgment but is the measure of his judgment; that this idea is of a kind that ought to be realized in law and action; that its violation is an injury, which his mind rejects as unreason; that this unreason is an offense not only against his own intelligence but against God, Who commands justice and forbids injustice.[1]

—Fr. John Courtney Murray, SJ 1960

Human rights developed in response to specific violations of human dignity, and can therefore be conceived as specifications of human dignity, their moral source.[2]

—Jürgen Habermas, 2012

Introduction

The Dominican friar Bartolomé de las Casas described the conquest, dispossession, and destruction of the lives and communities of the indigenous peoples of the New World in several of his historical works, including *A Short Account of the Destruction of the Indies*. Las Casas originally composed the work for the Emperor Charles V around 1542, but after Charles' abdication, presented the formal report to King Philip II of Spain. It was first printed in 1552. Earlier Las Casas had traveled to the New World as a member of the secular clergy and chaplain to Spanish settlers before returning to Spain and entering the Dominican Order. During his first experiences in the New World he was a settler on the island of Hispaniola where he had been granted land and an allotment of natives to work as slaves. He was moved by the preaching of Dominican Friar Antonio Montesinos, whose famous Christmas homily (1511) called on the Spanish settlers on Hispaniola to repent of their mistreatment of the native peoples and to restore them to freedom. However, Las Casas only relinquished his *encomienda* after his own meditation on a reading from the *Book of Sirach* (34, 21-22) in preparation for an Easter homily in 1514. The scriptural passage reads:

> Ill-gotten goods offered in sacrifice are tainted.
> Presents from the lawless do not win God's favor.

Later Las Casas returned to Spain with Montesinos and entered the Dominican Order. His actions on behalf of the peoples of the New World caused him to be named the official "Defender of the Indians" by the Council of the Indies, and to be appointed the Bishop of Chiapas.[3]

This paper opens with a prologue of two quotations from very different scholars engaged in very different inquiries. In Father John Courtney Murray's study of the natural law roots of the American political tradition, *We Hold These Truths: Catholic Reflections on the American Proposition*, Murray considered and described what he understood to be the empirical and practical essence of natural law in the context of a modern democratic society. One might even call it a phenomenological description of natural law. However complex and contested the metaphysical background of natural law may be, its application involves empirical claims. The empirical situation described is understood to be the consciousness of a hypothetical third party observer who witnesses an injustice done to another person. It is not sufficient to make the claim of injustice on the level of social convention, since the injustice arises from a formally valid law. Rather, the observer insists on the truth of the judgment against the party who has violated justice and injured the victim.[4] Notice, though, that the political situation described is one in which a person, or group of people, has been injured, harmed, and perhaps humiliated and dehumanized.

A half century later the German philosopher Jürgen Habermas is engaged in a contemporary academic discourse of human rights, and especially the struggle to arrive at a satisfactory historical and theoretical account of the concept of human rights. However, like Murray before him, Habermas comes to focus on the practical situation of a person who has suffered injustice. His view is that human rights have developed in response to specific violations of human dignity, and derive their moral content from the development of the concept of human dignity. His account relies on a genealogy of the concept of human dignity from ancient Roman and medieval Christian sources, but as re-imagined in Kant's categorical imperative and as applied through a system of coercive law under a democratic constitution.[5] Habermas argues in the language of John Rawls for a "realistic utopia" of human rights against Samuel Moyn's thesis in *The Last Utopia* that human rights is a recent concept, and against a range of contemporary academic works that claim to show that international human rights regimes have failed.[6] Despite their different contexts, foci, and fields of inquiry, both Murray and Habermas focus on the same practical situation, that of a person or a people who have been done an injustice, or have been deprived of their dignity, or have had their rights violated.[7]

A scriptural and prophetic accusation of injustice from the *Book of Sirach* seemed to have convinced Bartolomé de las Casas, and led him to repentance. However, his repentance also seems to follow from a personal realization of his violation of natural law and of the natural rights of the people he held as slaves. Las Casas's contemporary and fellow Dominican Francisco de Vitoria has often been credited (or blamed) with introducing the concept of subjective natural rights into Thomist natural law philosophy in the sixteenth century.[8] So in reading the *Brief Account,* we may ask: Was Las Casas engaged in a debate about natural law, or about subjective rights? In undertaking such an inquiry, one might be moved to develop either a "thesis of rupture" that portrays Las Casas as someone engaged in total intellectual break from medieval understandings of law and justice; or one might be moved to develop a "thesis of continuity" that portrays Las Casas as a kind of intellectual aqueduct through which medieval versions of the concept of subjective individual rights flow into the contemporary concept of human rights by way of intellectual influence.[9]

Neither approach would be satisfactory, in part because the question is not really to the point. Las Casas's views are firmly grounded in legal and theological principles that are medieval in origin and substance, and his understanding of natural human sociability seems logically incompatible with the individualism of the contemporary European and North American discourse on human rights. Nevertheless, the inquiry seems timely precisely because the first decades of the twenty-first century have seen the production of a growing body of historical research on the origin and concept of human rights, in part in reaction to the continued occurrence of human rights violations on a massive scale.[10]

Authors like Micheline Ishay and Michael Hayden trace important contributions to the history of human rights from ancient philosophical ethics and major world religious traditions through the contemporary era.[11] The concept of human rights thus conceived has a very long history indeed. However, until recently, a more common approach to the history of human rights identified their origins in the revolutionary natural rights liberalism of the seventeenth and eighteenth centuries. One might call this approach a long history of human rights. An excellent recent example of the long history is Lynne Hunt's study *Inventing Human Rights.* Hunt emphasizes the way that the language of human rights becomes "self-evident" through social diffusion of fictional portrayals of injustice in domestic novels, and through protests against the use of torture to elicit evidence in French courts of the late eighteenth century, both of which may have contributed to the rise of empathy in human society that grounds the self-evidence of human rights.[12]

Political theorist Jack Donnelly, on the other hand, rejects the idea that contemporary human rights standards are essentially the same as early modern natural rights. He stresses that universal human rights have a short history, that they should be understood not to require the metaphysical foundations of natural law or natural rights, and that they should be understood to arise from an overlapping consensus that began to be formed around the Universal Declaration of Human Rights after World War II.[13] Narrative histories like Mary Ann Glendon's study *A World Made New: Eleanor Roosevelt and the Universal Declaration of Human Rights*, and Elizabeth Borgwardt's *A New Deal for the World*, may be seen to provide support for this shorter history of human rights by describing the new struggle for a universal bill of rights in the context of the post-war era.[14]

Another recent approach to the history of human rights promotes the idea that the concept has a very short history, even shorter than the narrative put forward by Donnelly. Samuel Moyn's *The Last Utopia: Human Rights in History* argues the contemporary understanding of human rights does not arise until the late 1970s. Like Donnelly, Moyn insists that human rights be understood as a superordinate (and secular) concept of morality that allows individuals and minorities to challenge the sovereignty of the state. However, Moyn holds that human rights replaced other "utopias" through the language of international diplomacy only during the Carter administration, and through attempts to aid the cause of Soviet dissidents through the auspices of the Conference for Security and Cooperation in Europe.[15] Moyn's approach is that of a historian of international law and diplomacy, and the term "utopia" refers to any ideal that at some time is opposed to amoral realism in international politics.

Advocates of the short and very short histories of human rights occupy an intellectual terrain analogous to J.G.A. Pocock in his magisterial work on civic republicanism, *The Machiavellian Moment*,[16] in that they forcefully reject attempts to show continuity in the development of the concept of human rights, especially before the political revolutions of the eighteenth century, just as Pocock seeks to establish the fundamental discontinuity of political discourse before and after the crisis of politics in fifteenth century Florence. Donnelly, in particular, posits a concept of human rights that arises from an international consensus surrounding the adoption of the Universal Declaration of Human Rights in 1948. For theorists like Donnelly this "thesis of rupture" is not just a matter of historiography. Donnelly is determined to show that earlier philosophical constructs like natural law and natural rights involve metaphysical claims that are indefensible today and undermine the supposed moral consensus in favor of universal human rights.

Infused with a Rawlsian quest for an "overlapping consensus" in favor of "equal concern and respect" for every person through an international human rights regime, Donnelly seems to be all too willing to lay down a wide variety of discursive weapons that may be needed in the present age. The development of an international moral consensus in favor of human rights norms may be a practical necessity for the protection of human dignity around the world, but many people will find it logically inconsistent to base inalienable rights claims on a social consensus. After all, if one considers the empirical situations described by Murray and Habermas, the concept of human rights seems to arise precisely in social situations in which a consensus in favor of inhumanity has come into existence in a society. The contemporary solution of "political conceptions" of justice consequently ends up being no solution at all to the ongoing protection of human dignity through a human rights ethic, since the abuse of political rule, and the violation of natural law, will always be a threat to human rights. There are no utopias in political reality.

This study develops Cary J. Nederman's insight that a Ciceronian understanding of human equality formed the basis of Bartolomé de las Casas's defense of the peoples of the New World. In a brief chapter titled "Equality, Civilization and the American

Indians in the Writings of Las Casas," in his work *Worlds of Difference: European Discourses of Toleration, c.1100-1550*, Nederman provides an extraordinary survey of the way that Las Casas appropriated passages from Cicero's philosophical and rhetorical works throughout the whole body of his own historical and legal works in defense of the Indians.[17] However, whereas Nederman's *Worlds of Difference* is focused on discourses of tolerance and toleration, the present study will focus on discourses of rights, or more precisely, arguments about the violation of people's human rights under natural law.

It will be necessary to provide a clear summary of Nederman's interpretation of Las Casas's works since he concluded that Las Casas did not rely on the modern discourse of subjective natural rights. It will also be necessary to explain why I believe Las Casas's *Brief Account* can and should be viewed as a human rights document. This will be made clearer through comparisons between Las Casas's description of the Spanish tyranny over the peoples of the New World, both in terms of its content and reception, and the rise of the contemporary human rights regime in the aftermath of World War II. As is often the case with historical comparisons, my logic is that of analogy rather than influence. I will then conclude with a brief reflection on the importance of Las Casas's works for contemporary histories of the concept of human rights. My hope is to suggest a path towards a defensible and practically applicable doctrine of human rights that is neither ideological nor utopian. I would suggest that this path cannot be found without some reference to the earlier tradition of natural law, understood not primarily as a metaphysical doctrine but as an integral part of political morality and of legal argumentation.

Revisiting equality and civilization in the writings of Las Casas

Contemporary scholars of Las Casas tend to fall into two camps, those who emphasize his medieval legal sources[18] and those who emphasize the Thomist-Aristotelian philosophical framework of the Second Scholasticism in sixteenth century Spain.[19]

Nederman's work could then be said to break new ground because of his emphasis on Las Casas's appropriation of Cicero's arguments for natural human equality based on the rational capacity for knowledge and virtue. An important aspect of Nederman's approach is his ability to catalogue a significant list of references to Cicero in the major works of Las Casas, especially in the *Historia de las Indias*, the *Apologétca Historia* and his *Apologia* in the debate over the rights of the "Indians" at Valladolid in 1551, translated as *In Defense of the Indians*.[20] In these works Las Casas set out to describe in detail the early history of Spanish contact with the peoples of the New World, and to condemn the violent conquest and dispossession of the "Indians" against justifications based on the idea that they were natural slaves or culturally inferior to the Europeans.

Nederman's strategy in his work *Worlds of Difference: European Discourses on Toleration 1100-1550* is to establish that Las Casas referenced a variety of Cicero's works (including *De legibus*, *De officiis*, *De natura deorum*, and *Disputationes Tusculanum*) in constructing his argument that all people are human beings, and that they are naturally equal based on their capacity for reason, religion, and social intercourse. Perhaps more importantly for the present argument, Nederman is able to provide direct evidence of Las Casas arguing that human persons are *individually* equal. This is of some importance, since at first gloss Las Casas may be taken to be arguing for the equality of all human peoples and not for the equality of individual persons. So one might conclude that Las Casas viewed Cicero's conception of natural equality in terms of the Christian idea that each person is made in the image and likeness of God.[21]

Having established that Las Casas had appropriated a Ciceronian understanding of natural equality, Nederman turns to the related question of whether human beings living in rude and solitary conditions could truly be understood to have the capacity for reason and civilization. Las Casas provides ample detail of the reasonableness of the native cultures in his historical works. However, the empirical case is there bolstered by Cicero's famous account of social development presented in *De inventione* (I, 2-3) and repeated in the later philosophical works of the Roman statesman.[22] A key point about Las Casas's use of this account is that he clearly considered people without the liberal arts and living in rude and scattered societies to be in a state of "second nature" brought on by their culture and local circumstances under the conditions of original sin. Las Casas believed that human beings are naturally reasonable and capable of social intercourse and the search for the truth about God.[23] Consequently, in *De unico vocationis modo omnium gentium* (hereafter *The Only Way*), Las Casas argued that the Gospel should only be preached through peaceful exhortation, and he condemned the Spanish conquest as irrational and unnatural.[24] Since the peoples of the New World lived in their own republics with their own possessions, it was the Spanish conquerors who engaged in violent unreason.

Finally, Nederman explained that this emphasis on nonviolent interaction with the peoples of the New World amounted to a genuine theory of toleration. He summarizes Las Casas's views:

> If all people (and peoples) possess rudimentary reason and knowledge of God, as well as potential to partake in civilized association, then every nation must be left to follow its own "natural" and appropriate route to maturity. The use of coercive force—either to destroy supposedly incorrigible barbarians or to speed the process of cultural evolution—is wrong and self-defeating.[25]

That Las Casas based his theory of toleration on a conception of human equality is also clear from his insistence that the peoples of the New World would have been within their rights to wage war against the Europeans in self-defense. When the Spaniards presented themselves under the force of arms and attacked the Arawak and Taino peoples of the Antilles, they forfeited their right to peaceful society with them. This concept of toleration that is based on an assertion of human equality entails a concomitant assertion of the right of self-defense against violence and aggression.

A Short Account of the Destruction of the Indies: An Indictment of Tyranny and Cultural Depravity

If we return then to Habermas's statement about human rights, that they arise from specific violations of human dignity and that they can be understood as specifications of human dignity as their moral source, we may consider Las Casas's *Short Account* as a possible example of human rights discourse. Habermas's genealogy of the concept of human dignity locates its origin in a vague category of "Roman and Christian" sources, and argues that the concept of human rights as a specification of human dignity is dependent upon a Kantian and deontological conception of human autonomy and the categorical imperative (Habermas, 2012, Section 4.2).[26] However, Nederman's account of Las Casas's theory of toleration seems to me more useful, since human dignity and natural human equality are actually worked out with clear reference to the key passages in Cicero, rather than to classical Roman sources in general, and since both Cicero and Las Casas ground their understanding of human dignity in a framework of natural sociability, rather than on a concept of human autonomy abstracted from common experience.

Implicit in Habermas's deployment of John Rawls's concept of a "realistic utopia" of human rights is the notion that the specific type of violation of human dignity that gave rise to contemporary human rights discourse was the experience of genocide during World War II.[27] However, Raphael Lemkin, the pioneer of genocide studies, pointed out that genocide was an old evil with a new name. When approaching Las Casas's *Brief Account*, one must not get lost in the redundant style and gruesome content of the work. The preface of the work lays down a simple groundwork to understand it as an indictment against the Spaniards who led and conducted the conquest of the Indies, which he argues led to the "destruction" of whole peoples and their adaptations to the natural world they inhabited.[28] The fact that Las Casas did not have the term "genocide" at hand when describing the events of the late fifteenth and early sixteenth centuries should not prevent us from considering the possibility that his work could be interpreted as an early example of an indictment against the constellation of crimes that have come to be understood as genocide.[29]

Las Casas's account begins with the observation that the "destruction" of the peoples of the New World stemmed from two policies of the conquistadors: first, their decision to wage wars of conquest against them; and second, their practice of killing anyone who dared resist and of enslaving the surviving population for hard labor, focused especially on the mining of gold (Las Casas 1992, 12-13).[30] Las Casas describes these practices as "policies" undertaken by the governors of the colonies, so one might say that the violation of the natives' human dignity was an official act undertaken by colonial authorities acting on the basis of the legal claims of the Spanish monarchy.[31]

The work is organized both geographically and chronologically. The first two chapters deal with conquest of the island of Hispaniola (14-25) and are especially important and convincing since these accounts are based on Las Casas's firsthand experience of the conquest and of the primary figures involved in it.[32] We also have a fairly clear idea of the complete collapse of the native population of Hispaniola during the first fifty years of European colonization. Estimates of the indigenous population in 1492 vary widely, but we can say with some certitude that a population in the tens of thousands, and possibly as high as 400,000, was reduced to around 300 by 1540, that is, in less than 50 years. We will return to Las Casas's accounts of the Spanish wars of conquests on Hispaniola below.[33]

The work continues with brief chapters on the other Caribbean islands before turning to the "Mainland" and Nicaragua, then a series of chapters that chronicle the conquests of New Spain (Mexico, but also parts of Guatemala and Honduras), Guatemala, and the Yucatan. After a series of brief chapters on smaller provinces in what are now Mexico, Columbia, and Trinidad, Las Casas turns to the Kingdom of Venezuela, Florida, and the region of the Rio de la Plata. Finally, he recounts the conquest of Peru and the Kingdom of New Granada (Columbia) before a brief conclusion and summary of his case. It is amazing to reflect on this enormous colonial enterprise of exploration and conquest that occurred in less than 50 years.[34]

Scholars have noted that Las Casas's style in this work is repetitive, but this seems to be intentional as he lays out the pattern of destruction that is repeated in each incident of the conquest. The pattern to be discerned is that the Spaniards used military force and terror to establish tyrannical rule over the indigenous peoples. Even when the native rulers worked with Spaniards to provide them with gold, the Spanish settlers eventually ended up attacking and oppressing them. Leaving aside cases in which the Spaniards immediately attacked the natives under the force of arms, killing most of the men and enslaving the women and children, the pattern begins with peaceful interaction between the Spaniards and the indigenous people. Then someone or some group of settlers commits some outrage against the indigenous population. On Hispaniola for instance, one of the "kings" of the Taino communities, Guarionex, worked diligently to get his people to pay tribute to the conquistadors in the form of gold measured in gourds. Despite the king's peaceful cooperation, his wife was taken by Francisco Roldán, one of Columbus's officers, and raped. Guarionex decided to leave the settlement and accept self-imposed exile in a neighboring region. However, the Spanish pursued him there and attacked the local settlement violently until the residents were forced to reveal the king's refuge. The Spanish took Guarionex in chains and planned to carry him off to Spain, but all of the many characters in the story died in shipwreck and sank with a large cargo of gold (18-20).[35] Las Casas viewed this sea disaster as a judgment of God against the Spaniards.

The wars waged against the natives often are described as being punctuated by the use of public torture to terrorize the surviving population, especially when the natives had offered armed resistance against the conquistadors. At the outset of the work, for instance, Las Casas describes the way that leaders among the Taino on Hispaniola were "grilled" alive by a particularly cruel officer who had been given charge of the execution detail (15-16).[36] Subsequent to these wars of suppression, the Spaniards adopted a policy of killing many natives as a reprisal if a Spaniard should be killed.

In short, the Spaniards engaged in brutal and unjust wars that culminated in their usurpation of the rightful rule of the leaders of the native communities. Las Casas set out to establish as a matter of fact and law that the conquistadors were tyrants. They had unjustly established rule as usurpers and had ruled capriciously, violently, and without concern for the bodily or spiritual welfare of the people under their rule.

Given the assertion of tyranny, it is important to clarify issues of the legitimacy of civil rule in Las Casas's thought, as it is very complex. Las Casas, unlike some of his Dominican contemporaries who rejected papal claims to legal jurisdiction over the entire world, accepted the idea that rule over the lands in the New World were "donated" to the kingdoms of Aragon and Castile in the papal bull of Alexander VI, *Inter caetera* (1493). Nevertheless, he denied that this donation conferred either civil authority or property rights on the Spanish: neither the right to usurp the civil authority exercised by the rulers of the indigenous people, nor the right to the property of individual subjects. The purpose of the donation was to induce the indigenous populations to receive the Catholic faith, not to deprive them of their freedom or their property. Rather, as Queen Isabella had put it, the people of the Indies were "subjects and vassals" of the monarchy, and their rulers had a legal status analogous to European nobility.[37] Further, the Spanish colonists sent to the New World to claim the New World for the Spanish Empire were in no way authorized to wage war on and massacre the people they found there.[38]

Las Casas applies his views in an important chapter on New Spain, which includes his account of Cortés's conquest of Mexico City. Las Casas, referring to the legal practice called "requirement" (*requerimiento*), points out that when the native peoples did not immediately accept their commands, the Spaniards dubbed them "outlaws" and viewed them to be in rebellion against Spain. According to Las Casas, the first principle of law and government is that no one who is not a subject of a civil government can be understood to be in rebellion against it.[39] The tyranny thus established was extended through the practice of *encomienda,* the system whereby the Spaniards distributed land holdings and people to be held as slaves. The idea behind the practice was that it would facilitate the teaching of the Catholic faith, since each settler would have responsibility for a small number of people. However, as Las Casas points out, the *encomenderos* were mainly uneducated men, and they made no effort to provide friars or other religious access to the people they held as slaves.[40]

So, instead of peacefully evangelizing the peoples of the New World within their own communities and within their native cultural understanding, the Spaniards usurped the power of their civil governments and used military power and terror to impose a system of slavery that precipitated the destruction of the Indies. In his conclusion to the work, Las Casas praised Charles V for the New Laws that were issued in 1542, which date he took to be the height of the destruction in the New World.[41] However, Las Casas and his fellow bishops in New Spain were unable to oversee the effective implementation of the New Laws, which included a ban on the *encomienda*. So the progress Las Casas had made in legal reform had little real impact on the lived experiences of people in the New World.[42]

Near the end of the work Las Casas summarizes the policy of the conquest in New Granada, in contemporary northwest South America. The native peoples there were either provoked or simply attacked by men under arms, terrorized by public torture or execution, and then parceled out as slaves:

> After the initial carnage and mayhem of conquest the Spaniards, as we have indicated, invariably subject the indigenous peoples to the horrors of slavery we have depicted; to one blackguard will fall two hundred natives, to another three hundred. The strategy favored by the fiend in human shape in overall command of the territory is to parade a hundred of these poor wretches (and they answer his summons like lambs to the slaughter) and then behead them on the spot, while he warned the others, "I shall do the same to you if you do not

obey my commands to the letter or if you try to run away" (Las Casas 1992,124).⁴³

Here we have evidence that Las Casas's Ciceronian view of human development may have led him to believe that the policies pursued by the Spanish in the New World caused them to become inhumane and unreasonable; indeed, diabolic. The conquest created a depraved culture that destroyed the nations of the New World, when those nations could have followed a natural path to cultural advancement and human fulfillment in cooperation with the peaceful Christian evangelism that Las Casas had advocated.⁴⁴

Human Rights and the Crime of Genocide in the *Short Account*

May we say that Las Casas has given us a human rights document in the form of an account of the crime of genocide against numerous nations and tribal groups subjugated by the Spanish in the New World between 1492 and 1542? We must begin by acknowledging with Nederman that Las Casas does not seem to have adopted the early modern subjective natural rights framework often associated with Thomas Hobbes, much less the contemporary human rights framework advocated by Jack Donnelly, among others. As I noted above, this type of historical project requires that one work through arguments analogically and avoid claims of "influence" and direct correspondence of meaning that are made problematic by historiographical concerns about meaning and context. It is in response to these problems that Nederman's discussion of Las Casas's appropriation of Cicero's texts is very helpful. The ancient account of human sociability in Cicero provides us with a non-biblical and pre-Christian account of "fallen human nature."⁴⁵ As noted above, Las Casas's account of the behavior of the Spanish conquerors in the New World describes them as following policies that lead them into a "fallen condition." They become habitually violent, tyrannical, and destructive because they pursued policies that relied on violence, tyranny, and destruction.

Nederman's focus on Las Casas's description of cultural development, especially in the *Apologética Historia Sumaria*, traces the movement of a human society from "pre-rational modes of action" to a civilized state characterized by reason and law, based on the analogy to the way a human individual develops the use of reason as he or she grows in body and mind: "Las Casas's implication is clear: Ontogeny recapitulates phylogeny. Human Civilizations progress toward completion as they replace their animalistic standards of behavior with a set of rational precepts—social, political, legal, and religious."[46]

Las Casas's account of evangelization in *The Only Way* follows from this account and foresees people moving from a condition of savagery and wildness to a civilized state by "compelling the human intellect rationally."[47] We should acknowledge too that Las Casas was radical in the application of his principles. He insisted not only that the peoples of the New World had a natural right to resist aggression but also that the Spanish crown owed restitution for the destruction done by the wars of conquest and enslavement.[48]

However, one also must see that the process of cultural development in human society is not linear and unidirectional; depraved cultural practices lead to cultural decline, not progress. People living in the most advanced and humane culture might "fall" into inhumanity and unreason under social conditions like those experienced by the conquistadors. This point may be related to something that causes contemporary advocates of human rights standards embarrassment. They must constantly try to explain why we seem to learn of human rights through their violation. It also suggests a profound reason to avoid grounding human rights in any utopian ideological framework. Cultural change can transform a utopia into a dystopia, a republic into a tyranny.

Cicero's understanding of his own philosophical teaching is also interesting for our case. Cicero is often identified as a Stoic because of the content of his moral doctrines and his assertion of natural law, but he identified his own views with later Academic skepticism.[49] Therefore, he is an example of a person who was able to maintain and assert a conception of natural law that was not dependent on a dogmatic adherence to the paradoxical theological and metaphysical doctrines of the Stoics. That is to say, Cicero's work as a whole suggests a skeptical basis for a natural law tradition. For Cicero it is reasonable to treat all human beings as equal in dignity because they are all human beings, and therefore capable of forming a society on the basis of reason. As Nederman points out, Las Casas was more consistent in his promotion of Cicero's principles than was Cicero himself.[50] It may be that Las Casas's consistency is related to his adherence to the Christian view that human moral equality is grounded in the status of the human person made according to the image and likeness of God, but that theological doctrine is not integral to the case at hand.

If we approach the *Short Account* in this way we see that the work implies an account of human rights based on the principle that "all nations of the world are human beings." The right of the peoples of the New World, individually and collectively, to defend themselves against violent attack is quite evident in the author's repeated condemnation of the actions of the conquistadors. Arising from this by logical extension would be an assertion that the property rights of individual owners and the collective rights of communities to political self-determination were violated by the conduct of the conquest. To put that into the language of contemporary human rights norms, we might say that the conquest entailed the violation of the human rights of the peoples of the New World and numerous crimes of genocide against them. However, this may require accepting that human rights are not a super-ordinate moral concept, since the human rights we describe are identified through reasoning about justice, law, and the natural sociability of the human person.

Las Casas and Twenty-First Century Histories of Human Rights

To conclude, one must refer to some of the contemporary histories of human rights that are mentioned in the introduction to this argument, but I sense that I must first acknowledge two negative responses to the view of human rights that is in the early stages of gestation in this argument. One is that the view of human rights that I am constructing out of Las Casas is internally inconsistent, since the existence of individual human rights requires the prior existence of autonomous individuals. The view that human beings are naturally social animals precludes the existence of human rights, properly understood. The second negative response is that, properly understood, Las Casas is making an argument for Christian evangelization that is inconsistent with the toleration of cultural diversity, so that he should properly be condemned as a religious proselytizer and an enemy of human rights. I take these hypothetical responses to be serious problems for the communication of my approach, and so will hazard the beginning of a hypothetical reply to each.

The first issue arises from the claim that a concept of human rights cannot be logically consistent with an assertion of natural human sociability, since human rights are the rights of individuals. In fact, though, contemporary human rights advocates frequently struggle to construct an account of the empathy that would be sufficient to ground a principle of equal concern and respect for all people, or human dignity in Habermas's account, out of liberal individualism. The problem was observed by Jacques Maritain in his work *The Person and the Common Good*.[51] The origin of the problem is that the human individual is not just an individual, but an individual person; and a person is a being who lives in relations with other persons. That is to say, human experience is the experience of human social intercourse. Whether one approaches human society from the perspective of physical need, or the perspective of moral development, it should be obvious that part of what we mean by "human being" is a being that lives in society with other human beings. If the concept of human rights requires us to repudiate this observed phenomenon, it is not worth defending.

Richard Hiskes, a contemporary human rights theorist working on the problem of the universality in human rights norms, has made an ingenious argument to show that Thomas Hobbes's state of nature could be reinterpreted to describe an emergent human right of contract (Hiskes 2014).[52] Of course, one might retort that Hobbes identifies one natural right, the absolute liberty to do what is necessary to preserve one's own life, so that the "right" of contract in his argument is really a "duty" of the law of nature to seek peace. Nevertheless, Hiskes is on to something very important for the defense of human rights in a world of cultural diversity and conflict. Rights are best understood in terms of specific claims that emerge, or become substantial, in the context of a human society, and individual rights have a relational basis.[53] What Las Casas describes in *The Short Account* is the destruction of the life of a fully constituted human society and its replacement with a continuous war of tyranny over the indigenous populations of the New World. That is to say, sometimes Hobbes' *Leviathan* actually does not end war, but is war: the war of the powerful against the weak.

As to the problem of Las Casas's evangelical Christianity, one has to acknowledge that Las Casas's insistence on the legitimacy of the papal donation of authority (to preach the Gospel to the peoples of the New World) to the Spanish monarchy would seem to undermine his argument in favor of the freedom of the peoples of the New World. However, the problem is not the evangelical nature of Las Casas's Christianity. Rather, Las Casas was still living in the context of a persecuting society in which the application of the coercive power of the government to achieve religious orthodoxy was assumed.[54] Nevertheless, even during the most intolerant phases of the development of constitutional government in medieval and early modern Europe, individuals or institutions within the Catholic Church, including the papacy, religious orders, and universities, at times engaged in public opposition to individual rulers and particular policies. Las Casas struggled to get Charles V to accept the reforms outlined in the New Laws (1542-1543), only to have Charles abdicate his positions as Holy Roman Emperor and Spanish Emperor (1555). The ascension of Phillip II to the Spanish throne led not only to the repeal of key provisions of the legal reform (like the end of the *encomienda*), but also to the trial of Las Casas' close associate and fellow Dominican, Bartolomé Carranza de Miranda, Cardinal Archbishop of Toledo before the Spanish Inquisition.[55]

In the end, Las Casas's goal of peaceful evangelization is analogous to the goal of achieving an effective global consensus in favor of the protection of universal human rights norms against various kinds of contemporary persecution and tyranny, some religiously motivated, some entirely secular, but most a complex mixture of economic, political, and religious interests. The goals of contemporary human rights advocates are served by a careful consideration and adherence to Cicero's understanding of the way that reason and rhetoric can be instrumental in motivating people to peaceful fellowship:

> The interests of society, however, and its common bonds will best be conserved, if kindness be shown to each individual in proportion to the closeness of his relationship.
>
> But it seems that we must trace back to their ultimate sources the principles of fellowship and society that Nature has established among men. The first principle is that which is found in the connection subsisting between members of the human race; and that bond of connection is reason and speech, which by processes of teaching and learning, of communicating, discussing, and reasoning associate men together and unite them in a sort of natural fraternity (*De Officiis* I. 50).

Given this, it seems correct to think in terms of a very long history of human rights while recognizing that the concept defended here is of relatively recent origin. Justice, natural law, natural rights, and human rights are all concepts that might be deployed against a cultural or political system of legally grounded practices that dehumanize, injure, and destroy other people.

Notes

1. John Courtney Murray, SJ, *We Hold These Truths: Catholic Reflections on the American Proposition* with an introduction by Peter Augustine Lawler (Lanham, MD: Sheed & Ward, first published 1960, classic edition, 2005) 294.
2. Jürgen Habermas, "The Concept of Human Dignity and the Realistic Utopia of Human Rights," in *Philosophical Dimensions of Human Rights: Some Contemporary Views*, ed. by Claudio Corradetti (Springer International Publishing AG, 2012), 63-79, at 63.

3. All references are to Bartolomé de las Casas, *A Short Account of the Destruction of the Indies*, Trans. by Nigel Griffin with Introduction by Anthony Pagden, (New York and London: Penguin Books, 1992). This biographical information can be found in Anthony Pagden's introduction, xiii-xxx.
4. *We Hold These Truths…*, One cannot help but connect Murray's description of natural law with Aristotle's explanation of the role that the concept of the natural plays in forensic rhetoric when the written law is opposed to one's case (*Rhetoric* I, 15, 1375a25ff).
5. Habermas, "The Concept of Human Dignity…,' sections 4.2 and 4.3.
6. See Samuel Moyn, *The Last Utopia: Human Rights in History* (Cambridge, MA: Harvard University Press, 2010). While it is not clear that Habermas's genealogical approach is directed against Moyn's insistence on the very late arrival of the concepts of human dignity and human rights, Moyn does explicitly reject Habermas's genealogy of human dignity in his subsequent work, *Christian Human Rights* (Philadelphia: University of Pennsylvania Press, 2015), 188, n3.
7. I list injustice, indignity, and the violation of rights together to stress that they are in some sense cognate concepts linked through the reality of the harm done to a person or persons.
8. See Anabel S. Brett, *Liberty, Right and Nature: Individual Rights in Later Scholastic Thought* (Cambridge: Cambridge University Press, 2003); Brian Tierney, *The Idea of Natural Rights: Studies on Natural Rights, Natural Law and Church Law, 1150-1625* (Atlanta, GA: Emory University Press, 1989);and Richard Tuck, *Natural Right Theories: Their Origins and Development* (Cambridge: Cambridge University Press, 1982).
9. See Cary Nederman, *Lineages of European Political Thought: Explorations along the Medieval/Modern Divide from John of Salisbury to Hegel* (Washington: Catholic University Press, 2009).
10. Some scholars argue that international human rights law has been a failure. See Eric Posner, "The Twilight of Human Rights Law," opendemocracy.net 25 November 2014; and Emilie Hafner-Burton and Kiyoteru Tsutsui, "Justice Last: The Failure of International Human Rights Law to Matter Where Needed Most," *Journal of Peace Research* 44 (2007), 407-425, and "Human Rights in a Globalizing World: The Paradox of Empty Promises," *American Journal of Sociology* 110 (2005), 1373-1411.
11. Micheline Ishay, *The Human Rights Reader*, 2nd Edition (London: Routledge, 2007) and *The History of Human Rights From Ancient Times to the Globalization Era* (Berkeley: University of California Press, 2008). Also see *The Philosophy of Human Rights*, ed. by Patrick Hayden (St. Paul, MN: Paragon Press, 2001).
12. Lynn Hunt, *Inventing Human Rights: A History* (New York: W.W. Norton, 2007); Maurice Cranston (1967) "Human Rights: Real and Supposed" in Hayden; (2001), *The Philosophy of Human Rights*.

13. Donnelly, *Universal Human Rights in Theory and Practice*, Third Edition (Ithaca, NY: Cornell University Press, 2013).
14. Elizabeth Borgwardt, *A New Deal for the World: America's Vision for Human Rights* (Cambridge: Harvard University press, 2005); Mary Ann Glendon, *A World Made New* (New York: Random House, 2001).
15. Moyn, *The Last Utopia*.
16. J.G.A. Pocock, *The Machiavellian Moment: Florentine Political Thought and the Atlantic Republican Tradition* (Princeton: Princeton University Press, 1975).
17. Cary J. Nederman, *Worlds of Difference: European Discourses of Toleration, c.1100-1550* (University Park, PA: The Pennsylvania State University Press, 2000), 99-115. Nederman's approach is informed by Lewis Hanke's scholarship, and especially *All Mankind is One* (De Kalb, IL: Northern Illinois University Press, 1974), as both are focused on Las Casas's insistence on the Ciceronian principle that all human beings are united in the soul's capacity for intellectual reflection.
18. See Tierney, *The Idea of Natural Rights*; James Muldoon, *Popes, Lawyers and Infidels* (Philadelphia: University of Pennsylvania Press, 1979); and Kenneth J. Pennington, "Bartolomé de las Casas and the Tradition of Medieval Law," *Church History* 39 (1960), 149-161.
19. See Thomas O'Meara, O.P. "The Dominican School of Salamanca and the Spanish Conquest: Some Bibliographical Notes," *The Thomist* 56 (1992) 555-582; and Anthony Pagden, "Dispossessing the Barbarian: The Language of Spanish Thomism in the Debate over the Property Rights of the American Indians" in *The Languages of Political Theory in Early Modern Europe* ed. by Anthony Pagden (Cambridge: Cambridge University Press, 1987), 79-98, and *The Fall of Natural Man* (Cambridge: Cambridge University Press, 1986). There are also studies that dismiss Las Casas as a critic of the Spanish colonial enterprise from a post-colonialist perspective. See Daniel Castro, *Another Face of Empire: Bartolomé de Las Casas Indigenous Rights, and Ecclesiastical Imperialism* (Durham, NC: Duke University Press, 2007).
20. Bartolomé de las Casas, *In Defense of the Indians*, trans. by Stafford Poole, C.M. (De Kalb, IL: Northern Illinois University Press, 1974); *Historia de las Indias*, 3 Vols. Ed. Agustín Millares Carlo (México City: Fondo de Cultura Económica, 1951); and *Apologética Historia Sumaria*, 2 Vols. Ed. Edmundo O'Gorman (México City: Universidad Nacional Autonomía de México), 1967.
21. Nederman, *World of Difference*, 102-105.
22. Cicero, *De Inventione*, I, 2-3 in *De Inventione, De Optimo Genere, Topica*, Trans. by H.M. Hubbell (Cambridge, MA: Loeb Classical Library, 1949).
23. Here one may note that the distinction between elements of Las Casas's argumentation that are grounded in Cicero and those grounded in Thomistic the-

ology are not perfectly discreet categories. See *Summa Theologiae* I-II, 94, 2. In the body of his response, Aquinas uses a list of natural human inclinations that are almost certainly derived from Cicero's *De officiis* (I.11ff) to identify the varieties of natural law precepts.
24. See Las Casas, *The Only Way*, ed. by Helen Rand Parish and Trans. by Francis Patrick Sullivan, SJ (New York: Paulist Press, 1992).
25. Nederman, *Worlds of Difference*, 110-111.
26. Habermas, "The Concept of Human Dignity...," Section 4.2.
27. Moyn raises important questions about the contemporary tendency to assume the centrality of the Holocaust in the early movement for an international human rights declaration after World War II. See *Christian Human Rights*, especially Ch. 1, 25ff.
28. One of the most difficult parts of assessing the usefulness of Las Casas's arguments in the *Brief Account*, and in his complete *Historia de las Indias*, is the question of the reliability of his estimates of population and the collapse of population in the New World during the first fifty years after first contact with the Europeans. For a balanced account of the available demographic data see Gustavo Gutiérrez, "Appendix 1: The Demographic Question," in *Las Casas: In Search of the Poor of Jesus Christ* (Maryknoll, NY: Orbis Books, 1993), 461-464. In the end it is impossible to deny that, especially on the island of Haiti, the Spanish conquest resulted in the destruction of the population and the natural bases of human society as it existed before contact.
29. See Nederman "A Middle Path: Alexander Passerin D'Entreves" in *The Lineages of European Political Thought...*, 49-60. According to Nederman, D'Entreves argued that at times language can lag behind thought. Also see Raphael Lemkin, *Lemkin on Genocide* (ed.) Steven Leonard Jacobs, (Lanham, MD: Lexington Books, 2012), 20-21.
30. Las Casas, *A Short Account...*, 12-13.
31. As Francis Patrick Sullivan, SJ, has pointed out, Las Casas's sympathy for Columbus did not prevent him from blaming the "Old Admiral" for establishing this pattern of relations with the Tainos on Hispaniola. See Sullivan, *Indian Freedom: The Cause of Bartolomé de las Casas* (Kansas City, MO: Sheed & Ward, 1995), 17ff.
32. Las Casas, *A Short Account...*, 14-25.
33. See Gutiérrez, *In Search of the Poor...*, 462-63.
34. Las Casas, *A Short Account...*, 26-130.
35. *Ibid.*, 18-20.
36. *Ibid.*, 15-6.
37. For concise summary of this doctrine, based especially on Las Casas's final work, *On Royal Power* (*De Regia Potestate*), see Anthony Pagden's introduction to *A Short Account*, pp. xv-xvii. A summary of the work in translation is found in Sullivan, *Indian Freedom...*, 324-327.

38. Las Casas, *A Short Account*..., 52.
39. *Ibid.*, 52-3.
40. *Ibid.*, 126.
41. *Ibid.*, 127-30.
42. Helen Rand Parish provides a brief but useful discussion of the variety of political factors that made it impossible for the New Laws to be effectively enforced in her "Introduction: Las Casas's Spirituality—The Three Crises," in Las Casas, *The Only Way*, 9-58, see especially 41-54.
43. Las Casas, *A Short Account*..., 124.
44. Here it is useful to note a connection made by historian James H. McGregor between the Spanish colonial enterprises in the New World and the behavior of troops under the command of Emperor Charles V who carried out the invasion and sack of Rome in 1527: "The horrors visited on the New World were not unique to our hemisphere. Spanish troops did not throw away the rule book and run amok when they left Europe behind… What happened in Tenochtitlán in 1521 happened again in Rome in 1527." See McGregor's translation of Luigi Guicciardini's (1478-1551) account, *The Sack of Rome* (New York: Italica Press, 1993), Preface, ix.
45. See Cary J. Nederman, "Nature, Sin and the Origins of Society" *Journal of the History of Ideas* 49 (1988), 3-26; and Wood, Neal "Populares and Circumcelliones: The Vocabulary of 'Fallen Man' in Cicero and St. Augustine" *History of Political Thought* 7 (1986), 33-51. One should note, however, that Cicero's account of fallen nature is not posited as a universal human condition, and is therefore distinct from the Christian notion.
46. Nederman, *Worlds of Difference*..., 107.
47. *Ibid.*, 107-08.
48. *Ibid.*, 113, referencing Las Casas, *The Only Way*...., 158ff, in the edition by Helen Rand Parish.
49. In *Worlds of Difference*, Nederman applies this understanding of Ciceronian skepticism as a basis for natural law reasoning in a study of John of Salisbury, 39-52. For a more extensive study of Cicero's skepticism see J. C. Laursen, *The Politics of Skepticism in the Ancients, Montaigne, Hume and Kant* (Leiden: Brill, 1992). One should notice that this mode of philosophical skepticism must be distinguished from the contemporary tendency, identified by Pope Benedict XVI and Pope Francis, to deny that there are any indisputable truths to guide our lives. Cicero, John of Salisbury, and Las Casas all affirmed a real metaphysical order and a natural law morality. See James M. Jacobs, "The Rational Order of Nature and the Environmental Implications of Natural Law," *Lex Naturalis* 2 (2016), 65-86.
50. *Worlds of Difference*, 102.
51. Jacques Maritain, *The Person and the Common Good*, Trans. by John J. Fitzgerald (Notre Dame, IN: University of Notre Dame Press, 1966). The work

was originally published in 1946, and is in part a response to Neo-Thomistic philosophers like Charles de Konink who rejected Christian personalism as an attempt to import totalitarian existentialist or Marxist concepts into Catholic political thought. See Charles de Konink (1943), "The Primacy of the Common Good against the Personalists," in *The Writings of Charles de Konink*, ed. and trans. by Ralph McInerny (Notre Dame; University of Notre Dame Press, 2009), Volume II, 63-163.

52. Richard P. Hiskes "A Very Promising Species: From Hobbes to the Human Right to Water," in *The Human Rights Paradox: Universality and Its Discontents*, ed. by Steven J. Stern and Scott Strauss (Madison: University of Wisconsin Press, 2014), 224-245.
53. For a clarification of this point see Thomas Williams, *Who Is My Neighbor? Personalism and the Foundations of Human Rights* (Washington: Catholic University of America Press, 2005), 3-13.
54. See Robert Ian Moore, *The Formation of a Persecuting Society: Power and Deviance in Western Europe, 950-1250* (Oxford: Blackwell, 1987). The problem with Moore's approach, the unqualified assertion that no Christian in medieval Europe was an opponent of intolerance, is that it assumes that official policies of intolerance were successful and that "true" tolerance can only be derived from modern liberalism. This causes one to lose track of a variety of intellectual paths to tolerance that developed during the High Middle Ages and Renaissance, and of the new forms of official intolerance that could only have arisen with the higher level of organization and social control that exists in a modern state. For a more balanced approach see the studies in *Beyond the Persecuting Society: Religious Toleration before the Enlightenment*, ed. by John Christian Laursen and Cary J. Nederman (Philadelphia: University of Pennsylvania Press, 1998).
55. Parish, "Introduction: Las Casas' Spirituality…," 50-54. Parish notes that Las Casas considered the Spanish Inquisition of this period to be an arm of the Spanish monarchy, and that the manuscript of his treatise *On the Limits of Royal Power* was seized. The Inquisitors openly harassed him though they could not arrest him nor force him to testify because of his status as a bishop.

Review of *Philosophical Essays Concerning Human Families* by Stanley Vodraska (University Press of America, 2014)

Matthew Minerd

In this volume, Stanley Vodraska gathers together an important collection of reflections on themes pertinent to what might be called "familial moral philosophy," or, using a denomination taken from the categories of classical philosophy, "economics," understood as the moral-philosophical investigation of matters pertaining to the family as a natural society. Vodraska, likely unknown to most readers, was educated at St. John's University (Minnesota) and at the University of London, and also spent time as a Fulbright Scholar at *L'Institut supérieur de philosophie* at the University of Louvain and as a Woodrow Wilson Fellow at the University of Chicago. He taught philosophy for over forty years at Canisius College in Buffalo, New York. Vodraska's work on these matters deserves the reading of philosophers interested in matters pertaining to the natural law, for the texts collected herein represent a very thoughtful and erudite treatment of an often-overlooked, though vitally important, division of classical (and scholastic) moral philosophy.

At first glance, the initial essay in the volume appears to be a diatribe against a speech given in 2000 at Santa Clara University by Fr. Peter Hans Kolvenbach, S.J., who at that time was the superior general of the Society of Jesus. The speech was given at a conference on "Commitment to Justice in Jesuit Higher Education," and it occasioned Vodraska's criticism because of what the latter perceived to be a critical oversight in Kolvenbach's paper. Quite insightfully, Vodraska notes that the particular post-1975 vocation of the Society, being oriented as it is to "social justice" on the part of religious priests, does not present a univocal measure for the justice to be exercised by all people. Writing in an obviously Catholic context, Vodraska stresses that Fr. Kolvenbach's speech failed to speak to the justice claims that are unique to familial life.

While this first essay is a bit uneven and not purely "philosophical" in content, it raises the central issue for Vodraska's various essays, namely that the order of justice (as well as the theological order of charity) demands a moral vocabulary that can acknowledge that confamiliarity generates unique justice claims that at times (and rightly so) take precedence over supposed justice claims made by those who are more distantly related to us. The reader must work through this essay quite diligently to see with full clarity the implications and import of his argument, which risk being lost in his lengthy prose. In short, it is Vodraska's well-founded opinion that failure to explicitly account for "familial obligation," "familial justice," or (in Vodraska's felicitous phrase) "the Principle of Familial Preference," ultimately leads one to an egalitarianism that cannot account fully for a hierarchical ordering of ends or of inter-personal loves (into which familial preference fits as one unique, irreducible form of natural love).

The second essay, "Works of Mercy and the Principle of Familial Preference," helps to flesh out some of these claims, wherein Vodraska addresses the notion of family life as an important place for the practice of the virtues and works of mercy. In this chapter, he spends perhaps too much time reflecting upon the correct meaning of the parable of the Good Samaritan, distracting from the purely "philosophical" character of his reflections. Nonetheless, his concern in so doing is understandable, given that he writes as a Catholic author concerned to fight moral claims that would assert that universal (or egalitarian) obligations "bleach out" the important moral obligations (and virtue-structure) of familial life. Indeed, the chapter ends with some important reflections upon the natural right of families to practice familial preference, a claim that will undergo important developments in the fourth chapter of the text.

However, before addressing that chapter, we must note the important third chapter, "Natural Justice in Heterosexual Family life." Along with the fifth chapter of the text, this essay undertakes a set of philosophical reflections that are arguably of the greatest import within Thomistic Aristotelianism's account of natural law and the family. Here, Vodraska argues for an extended Aristotelian account of justice based upon the general notion of aiming "at the right by adaptations to another according to equality." To do this, he must extend the account given by Aquinas concerning the adaptation/adjustment required by cases of natural justice. In this essay, Vodraska focuses on two forms of justice of obvious importance for domestic life, namely "parental justice" and "domestic justice." The former pertains to the natural justice requirements of parents in "adjusting" themselves to their children, "undertaken to bring about the child's survival, family life, and appropriate mental life," all of which activities must be undertaken from a voluntary, stable disposition—that is, from a virtue that is a species of *justice* objectively irreducible to other forms of justice. Likewise, his consideration of "the domestic just" is a very honest (albeit perhaps too brief) account of how heterosexual duality entails a unique form of natural justice, one that helps to give a rational account to the notion of "natural marriage" once defended more vociferously (for example) by Catholics, a notion that is quite necessary for discussing the problematic nature of the equivocation latent in contemporary jurisprudential acceptance of claims asserting an equivalence between heterosexual and homosexual matrimonial unions.

Indeed, in providing these accounts, Vodraska opens space for the articulation of the objectively distinct species of natural justice that pertain, for example, to the political domain of rulers and subjects. However, that is not his immediate concern here. In the course of his discussions and in a much clearer fashion than in previous chapters, he draws out the implications of these natural forms of justice, their connections to the aforementioned "principle of familial preference," and some very important claims regarding how these connections help to correct modern political theory's congenital inability to acknowledge fully justice claims (and organic communities) that do not fit neatly in the individual-state dichotomy. The chapter closes with an interesting remark regarding Benedictinism and the practices of virtue, adding an interesting element to the discussions concerning the so-called "Benedict Option" popular in some Catholic and Orthodox circles.

The fourth chapter, "Man and the State, God and the Family," interestingly differs from the broader Aristotelian tradition regarding the order of priority between the family and the political community. In this chapter, Vodraska argues for the unorthodox conclusion (from a broadly Aristotelian perspective) that the political order is subordinate to the family. In so doing, he relies on the claim that the "city-state" is a product of human art (and hence is not natural in the same sense as the family). In this chapter, Vodraska perhaps is prey to a modern conception of the state, which does bear strong resemblances to the "instrumental" and "artful" as opposed to the moral-prudential. This perhaps flows from a deficiency in what Vodraska understands to be "natural," reducing it too much to the biological presuppositions for practical reasoning. This shortcoming is unfortunate (and a bit perplexing) given his sensitivity to the multivariance of prudence in the generally Thomistic tradition out of which he writes. In any case, Vodraska's assertions are thoughtful and well-reasoned, such that even a purist Aristotelian reader will gain much from engaging with this portion of the text.

In the fifth essay, Vodraska outlines the historical and systematic themes relevant to a treatment of "domestic prudence," the particular virtue of practical reasoning related to the natural ends of the heterosexual domestic union. The opening of this chapter provides an excellent outline of the history of the aforementioned tripartite division of moral philosophy, giving the reader a succinct overview of ancient, medieval, Renaissance, and modern thinkers' treatment of the theme of "familial ethics." While the chapter arguably digresses for too long on the Biblical account of Tobit as an example of aspects of domestic prudence, the chapter outlines and exemplifies well the character of domestic prudence as a unique form of practical reasoning (and hence as the experiential source for a unique moral discipline reflecting on the familial-moral life). Vodraska clearly envisions himself carrying forward incipient insights contained within Thomistic Aristotelianism, and arguably this chapter provides the single most important contribution of the entire volume.

The final essay in the collection is "Against Blackstone and the Concept of Marriage as a Contract." This chapter argues on behalf of understanding marriage from the perspective of the moral reality of oath-giving and the social status derived from such oath-giving (and oath-breaking). As has been his wont throughout the collection, Vodraska stresses the natural rights of family life and the familial common good as providing a unique and irreducible basis for the "economic" order. Like other essays in the collection, the content is a little "uneven," and Vodraska's claims likely force the point in two regards. From a purely philosophical point of view, his disjunction between (natural) familial union and (legal) matrimony arguably creates a dualism wherein civil law no longer can function as an organic manifestation of the natural justice establishing family life. (Thus, one weakens one's ability to root civil matrimony upon its natural law antecedents.) Secondly, he is perhaps too strong in asserting the claims of nature against ecclesiastical authority as well, rendering difficult the integration of natural marriage into any further sacramental-ecclesial account of matrimony. Granting these issues, I do believe that his zealous insistence follows from his laudable (and overwhelmingly correct) desire to articulate the familial order as being a unique common good establishing rights and obligations that must be carefully integrated into an account of natural and legal justice.

If I have been critical at points in this review, this has been because I think quite highly of Vodraska's work in this collection. One is always more critical of "one's own" than of those with whom little convergence exists. The great moral-philosophic domain of the "economic" or "familial" has arguably been gravely undertreated by natural law-friendly philosophers, even those Thomists who occasionally recognize its status among the branches of moral philosophy. Although Vodraska is perhaps an unknown figure for many readers, I think his essays should be digested by the broader community of those favorable to the natural law, for they represent the thoughtful and erudite reflections of a someone who quite clearly understands (and has well articulated) the importance of the irreducible order of family life in human morality.

Review of *Ethics in the Conflicts of Modernity: An Essay on Desire, Practical Reasoning, and Narrative* by **Alasdair MacIntyre** (Cambridge University Press, 2016)

James G. Hanink

Is the volume under review the last, and definitive, work of Alasdair MacIntyre? Perhaps, but MacIntyre tells us that we need to recognize that the narrative of a life seeking the good remains *incomplete*. How could it be otherwise? The excellent person, the *eudaimon*, appreciates that his or her life is always incomplete. Indeed, it is for this reason that the good life and our reflection on it, in the end, opens the way to natural theology.

Wherever this volume belongs in MacIntyre's *oeuvre*, it is sweeping in scope and painstaking in argumentation. Its first chapter explores the interplay of what we desire and what sort of good is worth desiring. There is, of course, deep disagreement about how the rational agent identifies both individual and common goods. Moreover, rational agents function in specific social contexts, and in his second chapter, MacIntyre contrasts the sharply differing social worlds of Hume, Aristotle, Aquinas, and Marx. In his third chapter, MacIntyre explores the allegedly context-free "Morality" that is the product of contemporary academic philosophy. "Morality," however, faces telling criticisms. Oscar Wilde contends that the aesthetic trumps the ethical; D. H. Lawrence insists that one should follow one's deepest feelings. Bernard Williams makes the most trenchant criticism of "Morality." He argues that one's pursuit of the good, in its inception, must reflect an individual and non-negotiable authenticity. In chapter four, MacIntyre engages Williams with special regard to his account of authenticity. In doing so, he contends that Aristotelian-Thomism gives a better account of practical reason, the social order in which it functions, and the goods to which it is ordered than does Williams. MacIntyre finds that Thomism (and Thomas moves beyond Aristotle) is able to say far more about the virtues and about happiness than can its competitors. We are to adjudicate among theories by examining their explanatory fruits. MacIntyre's last chapter takes the form of four narratives, each one the story of an admirable practical reasoner who achieved his or her singular moral coherence in contentious contexts.

To indicate the guiding themes of this volume can only signal its range and richness. There are, though, two fresh contributions which merit special mention. The first is MacIntyre's development of the role of consultation and collaboration. Practical reasoning demands context; context, in turn, calls for sociologically educated analysis. Such analysis underscores the practical reasoner's need to take counsel with all whose voice is relevant. But to take counsel with others requires truth-telling. Absent honesty, there is no taking counsel. Absent counsel, there is no practical reasoning. But without practical reasoning, there is no flourishing, whether for the individual person or for the community. Yet more than truth is necessary. So, too, is the exclusion of force and fraud: "Without unconditional obedience to such precepts there cannot be shared deliberation [nor] rational agents" (56-57).

Here we can look to St. Thomas for confirmation. Prudence is at once a moral and an intellectual virtue. Counsel, moreover, is conjoined with prudence. Thomas presents counsel (*euboulia*) "as directed to prudence as to a principal virtue, without which it would be no virtue at all, even as neither are the moral virtues without prudence, nor the other virtues without charity" (*ST* II-II, q. 51, a. 2). Citing the Damascene with approval, Thomas observes that "counsel is *appetite based on inquiry*, so as to show that counsel belongs, in a way, both to the will, on whose behalf and by whose impulsion the inquiry is made, and to the reason that executes the inquiry" (*ST* I-II, q. 14, a.1).

The second fresh contribution is MacIntyre's welcome remarks on distributivism. He locates it in the social teaching of Leo XIII's Thomist revival, and he specifically contrasts distributivism with Marxism. In practice, Marxists fail to redress the perilous centralization of power in Communist states. Distributivists, however, emphasize the subsidiarity of local initiatives and dispersed authority. As both personalist and communitarian, they look beyond class struggle and welcome a vibrant civil society. Distributivists also reject capitalism's distortion of desires and its consequent undermining of practical reason. The result, MacIntyre writes, is that far too often what people want what "they have no good reason to want" (108). To what extent distributivism will succeed remains an open question. If it does succeed, it will do so despite its being at odds with the dominant structures of the day.

A great strength of MacIntyre's project is his eagerness to engage critics. So licensed, I will introduce a pair of objections to his latest work. The first objection is to his treatment of a key element of practical reason: the agent's rank ordering of competing goods. MacIntyre explicitly discusses rank ordering over twenty times in his text, and yet the term does not appear in its Index. I do not fault him for this, nor do I question his sympathetic elucidations of the social contexts in which an agent rank orders competing goods. My objection, rather, is one that a "new natural law" thinker would put forward. Though MacIntyre recognizes goods that are critical for human flourishing, his treatment of rank ordering could be more focused and cogent if he better distinguished between the incommensurable and non-fungible basic goods (that is, knowledge, truth, beauty, sexual union and child rearing, friendship, play, and life itself) and the instrumental auxiliary goods. By auxiliary goods, I mean the material and cultural preconditions that are necessary if we are to realize the basic goods. Indeed, this same distinction comes into play in understanding the common good as the coordination of basic and auxiliary goods.

MacIntyre's account of rank ordering would also be richer if he introduced the role of vocation. Doing so would draw him into theological reflection, and perhaps he deliberately chose not to pursue theology at this point. Yet surely his educated critics already realize that for Thomas the natural law, for us, is our way of participating in God's eternal law. The richness of vocation (and charism) merits full recognition in the rank ordering of goods.

In turning to my second objection, I readily acknowledge that another of MacIntyre's great strengths is his willingness to address the hard questions of a given culture. His ability to link such questions with core philosophical issues is unsurpassed, and his analysis of the ethics of modernity in terms of disparate views of practical reason is a case in point. Nonetheless, hard questions often begin with hard cases. MacIntyre introduces two "[t]echnicolor examples." In the first, I alone can prevent a terrorist's lethal attack on innocent people, but I can only do so by torturing the terrorist. In the second, I alone can stop a runaway vehicle from killing many innocent people, but I can only do so by killing an innocent bystander. MacIntyre notes that "Morality" does not lead us to shared convictions on how to act in such cases. True enough, but neither does his own natural law perspective. He highlights the absolute character of its negative prohibitions, and yet upon presenting us with this pair of cases, he does not propose to resolve them by saying that to deliberately kill the innocent is always wrong, as is assaulting anyone's core bodily integrity and capacity to reason.

Sometimes, too, the hard questions are ones of complicity. In totalitarian regimes millions of people compartmentalize their lives to advance their private goods—and think that they are right to do. They put aside, MacIntyre observes, "dreadful possibilities," and "do not care enough about the good as good to be outraged, even if quietly outraged, by the bad and the evil" (262, 310). MacIntyre is doubtless outraged by the deliberate killing of preborn human beings. Still, in a volume so penetrating as this one and given the entrenched practice of abortion, some readers might wish that he had shown public outrage at its advocacy by familiar elites.

That said, we can expect that MacIntyre will come to address whatever objections he meets. It is noteworthy that he closes this extended essay with the insistence that our lives, however well ordered to finite goods, make sense only in light of a final good that transcends them. His last words are a frank admission: "Here the enquiries of politics and ethics end. Here natural theology begins" (315).

CONTRIBUTORS

Paul J. Cornish is an associate professor of Political Science at Grand Valley State University. He holds a Ph.D. from The State University of New York at Buffalo and has published works on the political thought of St. Augustine, St. Thomas Aquinas and the later natural law tradition. His work has appeared in *The Review of Politics, European Journal of Political Theory,* and *Vera Lex.*

James G. Hanink received a Ph.D. in Philosophy from Michigan State University. His dissertation—*Persons, Rights, and the Problem of Abortion*—was written under the direction of Rhoda Kotzin. From 1976 until 2015, he taught at Loyola Marymount University in Los Angeles. He has published papers on ethics, social philosophy, epistemology, and metaphysics. He has been active in University Faculty for Life, the American Maritain Association, and the American Solidarity Party. He is also a contributing editor for the *New Oxford Review.* Now an independent scholar, his custom is to reflect often on the words of G. K. Chesterton, "Angels fly because they take themselves lightly." His wife, Elizabeth, and their children and grandchildren, urge him to do so more often.

James M. Jacobs is a professor of Philosophy and Assistant Academic Dean at Notre Dame Seminary in New Orleans, LA, where he has taught since 2003. He holds a B.A. from Harvard University and a Ph.D. from Fordham University. His major area of research is Thomistic natural law theory and more generally the need for philosophical realism as a response to modern nominalism and skepticism. He has had essays published in such journals as the *American Catholic Philosophical Quarterly, International Philosophical Quarterly, Nova et Vetera,* and *Heythrop Journal.*

Nathan Metzger is an adjunct instructor of Philosophy in Fordham University's School of Professional and Continuing Studies. He lives in Queens with his wife and four children.

Matthew Minerd, Ph.L, is a Ph.D. candidate in philosophy at The Catholic University of America. He is an adjunct professor of philosophy at Mount St. Mary's University in Emmitsburg, Maryland.

Scott Jude Roniger is a doctoral candidate in philosophy at The Catholic University of America. He holds graduate degrees in philosophy from the University of Chicago and the Pontifical University of the Holy Cross in Rome, and he has also published on Aristotle's *Metaphysics*.

Christopher Tollefsen is College of Arts and Sciences Distinguished Professor of Philosophy at the University of South Carolina; he has twice been a Visiting Fellow in the James Madison Program at Princeton University. He is the author, co-author, or editor of six books, including most recently *Lying and Christian Ethics* (Cambridge University Press, 2014). His book *Embryo: A Defense of Human Life*, co-authored with Robert P. George, was reviewed positively in *The New York Times*, *The Washington Post*, and elsewhere. Tollefsen is a member of the editorial boards of *The Journal of Medicine and Philosophy*, and *Christian Bioethics*, and is a regular contributor to *Public Discourse*.

CALL FOR PAPERS: Volume 4, 2019

We are accepting proposals for *Lex Naturalis* Volume 4, 2019. All topics related to natural law are welcome, especially those that relate natural lawand the founding documents of the United States

Abstracts (300-500 words) are due by May 31, 2018. Completed papers (25-30 pages) are due by August 15, 2018.

All submissions should be sent as an email attachment to Walter Raubicheck, Editor, at wraubicheck@pace.edu

Contributors
Address all submissions and correspondence to The Editor, LEX NATURALIS, Pace University, Department of Philosophy & Religious Studies, 1 Pace Plaza, New York, NY 10038. Please send two copies of the paper submitted. Include adequate margins, double space everything (text, notes, works cited, quotations). Use U.S. spelling and punctuation style (e.g. periods inside quotation marks; "double quotes" for opening and closing quotations). *The University of Chicago Manual of Style, 17th Edition,* is to be consulted regarding matters of style. Notes are to be numbered consecutively (in Arabic numerals) and placed at the bottom of the page.

Subscribers
LEX NATURALIS is published annually by Pace University Press, 41 Park Row, Room 1510, New York, NY 10038. Subscription price: $40. Please send all subscription inquiries to: PaceUP@pace.edu

Issues of *Vera Lex* are still available, including:
Volume 2, Numbers 1 & 2 (Winter 2001)
In this issue: Liberalism and Natural Law

Volume 4, Numbers 1 & 2 (Winter 2003)
In this issue: Feminism and Natural Law
(Annotated Bibliography)

Volume 6, Numbers 1 & 2 (Winter 2005)
In this issue: The Work of John Finnis

To order, go to www.pace.edu/press and use this discount code: VLp 2018 to receive a 20% discount through August 1, 2018, on these volumes.

www.ingramcontent.com/pod-product-compliance
Lightning Source LLC
Chambersburg PA
CBHW070837020526
44114CB00041B/1942